I THOUGHT I LOST

ANGELA CLEMMONS

COPYRIGHT ©2024 ALL RIGHTS RESERVED.

NO PART OF THIS PUBLICATION MAY BE REPRODUCED, STORED IN A RETRIEVAL SYSTEM, OR TRANSMITTED IN ANY FORM OR BY ANY MEANS, ELECTRONIC, MECHANICAL, PHOTOCOPY, RECORDING, OR ANY OTHER, WITHOUT THE PRIOR WRITTEN PERMISSION OF THE AUTHOR.

Published by: H.E.R.S. ON PURPOSE, LLC

FOREWORD

Of my niece, whom I love and respect for her ability to hear the Spirit of the Lord and follow His instructions, it is an honor to write the Foreword for her book.

As I read her book, the first thing I felt was that this is a true book of deliverance. Reflecting on the scriptures and their meanings, I sensed that the Spirit of the Lord is present throughout this work.

Some might think that this book is for teenagers, but it is for anyone seeking true deliverance. This book is for those ready to pivot in their lives. When Angela was fifteen, I asked her about her plans after high school. She smiled with her million-dollar smile and said, "I will be graduating within two years, Auntie. Then I'm going into the service, and after that, I will go to college. Then I'm getting married, and in two years, I will have children." To me, Angela knew her destiny and followed it. Although the path was different than what she planned, the destination was purpose.

Jeremiah 29:11 says, "For I know the plans I have for you," says the LORD. "They are plans for good and not for disaster, to give you a future and a hope." Angela, I am godly proud of you. Continue to walk in His plans and the hope the Lord has for you. You are fulfilling your divine purpose.

Prophetess Wanetta Ash

DEDICATION

To my grandmother, the late Irene Ash:

You were more than a praying woman and a Godly presence; you were a pillar in the community and a writer who fearlessly shared your life story. Your strong faith and the legacy you left behind inspire me every day. I continue your legacy as a Godly woman, sharing my story of overcoming and proclaiming the goodness and power of Jesus to others.

I know you smile down on me from Heaven, grandmother, as I embark on this journey to share my own story of overcoming. To the women who may not yet see their purpose, I dedicate this book to you. It's never too late to step into God's calling for your life. It's never too late to dream and to believe in the strength that lies within you. Through these words, I hope to encourage you that with God on your side, you cannot fail.

ACKNOWLEDGEMENTS

First and foremost, I would like to acknowledge Almighty God for choosing me before my mother knew me. Thank you, Lord, for keeping me through every test and trial. These tests have become testimonies that tell the world how good You are.

I would also like to express my deepest gratitude to my sister and friend, Weiner Crumbly, for her incredible vision and passion for authorship. Four years ago, she encouraged me to share a snippet of my story in the anthology "Overcomer." This single act sparked a fire within me that has only grown stronger with time. Weiner's unyielding dedication to helping women tell their stories has been a source of inspiration for me. Thank you, Weiner, for igniting that fire. There is so much more to come.

A special thank you to my coach, Dr. Enaysha Thompson, who played a pivotal role in helping me complete this book. I appreciate your efforts in keeping me accountable to deadlines, staying focused, and providing insightful perspectives on the bigger picture. Your guidance has been invaluable, and I am excited for what the future holds.

To my beloved family, thank you to my three daughters, my first reason for purpose. You are my inspiration. And to my husband, thank you for supporting me as I worked through this entire process. I may have seemed isolated, but I was truly focused. I appreciate your love and support throughout.

To my mother, thank you for giving me a strong foundation that has been integral in becoming who I am today. It was your love, understanding, and spiritual guidance that gave me the basis to stand firm. Your influence has been lasting and continues to guide me.

A heartfelt thank you to my Aunt Wanetta for listening to the Holy Spirit and sharing a word from the Lord with me that changed the direction of my life. As it is written, "Believe in the Lord your God, so shall ye be established; believe His prophets, so shall ye prosper."

Finally, I am deeply grateful for all the Lord is about to do through this work. May it be a blessing to everyone who reads it, and may it bring glory to His name.

Supporting Business

Rozlyn Sorrell / CEO

Vocal Precision Studio, LLC

www.vocalprecision.com

Paulette Moore

Purpose & Passion Skincare and More

www.Marypam1766Kay.com/

Sharon Hilton

Sharon's Sweet Stuff

www.Sharonssweetstuff.com

Leann Foster

EUTHENICS Foster Professional Development

Media Personality & Host of The Loving LeAnn Show

TABLE OF CONTENTS

Introduction 1

Chapter 1: The First Attempt 2

Chapter 2: Undesirable Influence 14

Chapter 3: Innocence Lost 28

Chapter 4: New Influence 41

Chapter 5: War Did Not Stop Me 55

Chapter 6: Through the Storm 68

Chapter 7: It Got Physical 83

Chapter 8: Lost Identity Finding Myself 97

Chapter 9: Purpose Discovered 110

Chapter 10: We Win – In the End 125

INTRODUCTION

Being completely transparent, my life has been marked by a myriad of experiences. Seasons of pain, depression, doubt, and disappointment have shaped my journey. Yet, amid these trials, each challenge became a stepping stone, and each setback, a lesson. I stand before you as a testament to resilience—not because my journey has been free of struggles, but because I have emerged stronger through it all.

My life is far from perfect. There have been complex situations that tested my spirit and moments that required every ounce of my strength to overcome. The journey was often exhausting, filled with instances where giving up seemed easier than pressing on. Yet, I fought through, discovering a strength within myself that I never knew existed. It's true what they say: the things that don't break you tend to make you stronger. Imperfect and flawed as I am, I find grace and guidance in Psalm 37:23, "The steps of a good man are ordered by the Lord: and He delighteth in his way."

God has always ordered my steps. Even when life didn't follow my dreams or plans, I found peace as I journeyed toward my purpose. Isaiah 49:1 declares, "Before I was born, the Lord called me; from my mother's womb he has spoken my name." This scripture illuminates the fact that God had a purpose for my life even before I discovered it. Though it was ordained for me and ingrained within me, it would be years before I truly understood and embraced it.

The enemy is well aware that there is a divine purpose for each of us, and his plan is to destroy it. His tactics are designed to derail us from our God-given destiny. As I reflect on my journey, I see how many times the devil tried to destroy me to abort my purpose.

Through the dangers of war, the peer pressure that led to destructive decisions, and my naiveté that caused me to give up my innocence as a young teenager, the devil used these as weapons. Depression, anxiety, and thoughts of suicide were tools to break my spirit. Physical attacks came, attempting to silence my voice. But despite these adversities, I have learned a powerful truth: when God has a purpose for your life, no enemy can prevent it. Though many weapons were formed against me, they did not prevail. God's plan for my life was indestructible.

Revelation 12:11 (NIV) reminds us, "They triumphed over him by the blood of the Lamb and the word of their testimony." I have authored this book to tell you how I overcame the devil's schemes and lies. This is a victorious testimony. My hope is that my story becomes a source of strength, confidence, and boldness for you. Recognize that, like me, you too are victorious! Allow the power within these pages to inspire you to embrace your resilience and triumph over adversities. Through my shared stories, may you find the courage to face your challenges with unwavering faith, assured that God's plan for your life is one of victory and restoration.

This book is an invitation to join me on a journey of faith, fight, resilience, and restoration. It is a testament that no matter how dark the night, dawn always follows. You may discover that some of my experiences mirror your own emotions and trials. Life's challenges can make us feel isolated, but I assure you, you have never been alone. God has always been with you. As you read about these real-life events, find strength in knowing that overcoming is possible. Use the devotions to help build your faith and discover your own method of triumph. This journey is not just mine but ours, and through faith and perseverance, you too can find victory in your life.

Devotional: Trusting God's Guidance in Every Step

Scripture Reading: Psalm 37:23-24 (NIV)

"The Lord makes firm the steps of the one who delights in Him: though he may stumble, he will not fall, for the Lord upholds him with his hand."

Psalm 37 is packed with powerful truths that help us confidently walk in victory. Reflecting on Psalm 37:23-24, I'm reminded that every step of my journey has been guided by the Lord. Looking back, it's clear that every trial and victory has been meticulously ordered by God. My life has seen pain, doubt, and disappointment. There were moments when the weight of depression and heartbreak seemed insurmountable, but each struggle was not the end, but a stepping stone.

I remember a particular time when I applied for a promotion at work. My credentials and work ethic were strong, and I put in significant effort to excel in my role. However, despite my qualifications, a friend was given the promotion instead of me. I was deeply disappointed and struggled to understand why I wasn't selected, leading me to second-guess myself.

In that moment of disappointment, a scripture my father taught me many years ago came to mind. Proverbs 3:5-6 reminds us to trust in the Lord and lean not on our own understanding. Even though it seemed like I had done everything right to earn the promotion, it was clear that it wasn't God's timing. At that moment, I remembered that I had to trust God.

In life's challenges and uncertainty, Psalm 37 offers hope and assurance. It reminds us of God's faithfulness and the comfort found in His promises. When we delight in Him, He gives us the desires of our hearts. Often, we seek immediate change, but this passage teaches the value of patiently waiting on God.

Life often leads us down unexpected paths, diverging from our dreams and plans. Yet, these detours build our faith and endurance. Each setback is a divine setup for a comeback. Though we fall, we can rise again, for His grace is sufficient, and His strength is made perfect in our weakness. Knowing that God directs our steps, even when we falter, is comforting.

Heartfelt Reflections

As you meditate on Psalm 37, think about the wisdom and comfort it offers. This passage reminds us of God's faithfulness and the beauty of patience and strength we receive when we trust in Him.

Read: Psalm 37 slowly and attentively.

Reflect: What verse(s) resonate with you today? What do they reveal about your current journey or challenges?

Respond: Write down your thoughts, feelings, and prayers. Pour out your heart onto these pages.

Rejoice: Rest on the promises in this Psalm. Thank God for what He has done, and what He will do according to His word! Allow these promises to bring you peace and hope today!

Prayer

Dear Lord,

Thank you for ordering my steps according to your perfect plan. I trust you with all my heart, knowing that your thoughts toward me are of peace, to give me a future and a hope. When I stumble, you uphold me. Through you, I live a life of total victory. In Jesus' name, Amen.

Chapter 1

The First Attempt

CHAPTER 1

The First Attempt

As a little girl, I was very inquisitive, fascinated by the mechanics of how things worked. My family might have considered me a Curious George! Being an only child until the age of nine, I had to entertain myself most of the time. I loved playing with my dolls, especially the big Barbie head. You couldn't tell me I wasn't a hairdresser! I even concocted my own makeup using Eucerin skin cream and water paint. Yes, I was quite creative. Coloring books, paper dolls, and spending hours outside, enjoying the fresh air and sunshine, were also my favorite pastimes.

These activities were my companions, filling the many moments of loneliness that come with being an only child. My mother told me I would have episodes of anxiety whenever a playmate came to visit and would throw dramatic fits of crying when they left. Thankfully, I had lots of first cousins, and in my eyes, I was very lucky. Some of the most exciting times of my childhood were spent having fun with them, playing games like jacks, hopscotch, and "Mother, May I?" Oh, how I loved going to the recreation center and playing Mancala (which we called marbles). My mother drove the city bus, and sometimes my cousins and I got to ride around town with her, which was always a thrill. Yet, the moments I treasured most were the times spent with my grandmother and grandpa in Alabama. My cousins were there also, compounding the fun!

Grandmother had huge pecan trees that provided endless delight as we gathered pecans to crack and devour. She would spoil us with her homemade biscuits, warm and melt-in-your-mouth scrumptious; straight from the oven. The summers were hot, and a highlight for us was the sweet, juicy watermelon we gobbled down while in the front yard, spitting out seeds and laughing in the Alabama sun. Those moments with my cousins brought laughter, adventure, and a sense of belonging. It was like having sisters and brothers. They were my playmates and best friends, making my childhood brighter whenever they were around.

My mother was single, having divorced at a young age. She had to work hard to provide for me, which meant she couldn't always be there. On those occasions, I was taken to my aunt's house for care. When my aunts needed a sitter, they called my mom. We had a small village where everyone was taken care of. If my aunts wanted to go out, they sent their children to my house for my mother to watch. Conversely, when my mother wanted to go out, I was sent back to my aunt's house, quick, fast, and in a hurry. It didn't matter whose house I went to, as long as I had someone to play with, I was happy.

Among these beautiful childhood memories, there were moments of real danger. One such instance stands out vividly in my mind. The first time the devil tried to kill me, I was about five years old. It was a normal day, and my little cousin Tony came over to play while his mother was working. He was a few years younger than me, which made me the BOSS. Having a younger person around made me feel big!

My mother said that whenever there was company, I was the 'Ringleader,' always stirring up mischief. On this day, we were watching TV, but my inquisitive nature was stewing for something new. The house was canvassed as I searched for my next exploit, and my attention was drawn to the electrical outlet.

At the tender age of five, fear was unknown. Minds at that age are sponges, soaking up environments and learning from every encounter. Watching my mom plug in lights and the iron countless times was a source of amazement at how simple actions could bring things to life. That day, a lone hairpin on the floor caught my eye. My curiosity got the better of me. What if I stuck the hairpin into the socket, I wondered? Would it produce power for me?

The moment I dared to insert the hairpin; the room filled with a deafening BOOM! The sound was like thunder, shaking the very walls. The force threw me backward, scaring my cousin Tony so badly that he darted from the room screaming. That day revealed what happens when a hairpin is stuck into a socket; you get stunned by a high-voltage jolt, and worse, charred fingers. My hand was fried and blackened; the hairpin a burnt reminder.

I lay there in shock, unable to process what had just happened. The smell of burnt skin and metal filled the air, making me sick to my stomach. My heart pounded, driving home the reality of my actions. Just moments before, I was a fearless child, driven by curiosity. Now, fear entered my life for the first time.

My mother rushed in, her face a mix of shock and relief. She saw how close I had come to disaster. Seeing her daughter lying there, she understood the gravity of the situation immediately. Realizing how close we were to tragedy, she whispered, "I couldn't even whip you for this, because you have already been beaten." This close brush with disaster left a lasting reminder of how a child's inquisitiveness can sometimes lead to jeopardy.

I now know that depending on the voltage and length of contact time, electric shock injuries in children can cause anything from minor discomfort to severe injury or even death. Reflecting on that day, I am grateful that the hairpin didn't take me out. My life had barely begun, and already I had faced an attack from unseen forces. But God protected me! Isaiah 54:17 (NIV) says: "No weapon that is forged against you will prevail, and you will refute every tongue that accuses you."

Even though I was too young to fully comprehend faith, God's divine protection was already at work in my life. Though I did not know God, I had a praying grandmother whose faith interceded for me. I vividly recall spending cherished moments with her as a child, being showered with love and soaking up wisdom. She would take me to church, teach me to cook, and show me the art of washing clothes and hanging them on the clothesline.

But what I remember most was her constant devotion to prayer. I can still hear her soothing voice as she fervently prayed for me. "She's your child," she would declare, calling out to Almighty God on my behalf. Grandmother was a praying woman. I saw her reading the

Bible and placing it under her pillow at night. When she prayed for me, she would ask the Lord to keep a "hedge" around me. I know in my soul that my grandmother's prayers added a divine hedge of protection.

For all the praying grandmothers reading this book, recognize the remarkable influence of your prayers! Your petitions to God create a fortress around your grandchildren, shielding them from dangers seen and unseen. A grandmother's prayers contribute to a legacy of faith for her grandchildren. Consistently and persistently lift their names to heaven, asking God for His divine protection and intervention. Your prayers are not in vain but hold power that will affect their destinies.

I thank God for my grandmothers, who prayed and interceded for me. Prayers filled with the power of God's word help direct our paths. I am a testament to the power of a grandmother's fervent prayers. Reflecting on that day, I am reminded of the powerful truth in Jeremiah 1:5 (NIV) "Before I formed you in the womb I knew you, before you were born, I set you apart."

From the moment I was conceived, God knew me and had a purpose for my life. The devil's plans and schemes could not change that. There was a divine purpose set in motion at my birth, a destiny I am meant to fulfill. The devil had an evil plan, but not this time! God, in His grace and mercy, stood between me and inevitable danger. He kept me! As I come to the end of this chapter, I want you to grasp the truth that there is an incredible purpose set in motion at your birth – a destiny you must fulfill. Despite the attacks the devil may have tried to derail you, they won't prevail. If you are reading this book today, it is not by sheer happenstance. It is because God has undeniably kept you too! Remember, no forces formed against you will prosper. Like Jeremiah, before you were ever born, God KNEW you. God CHOSE you, and there is a PURPOSE for you to fulfill!

Angela Clemmons

Chapter 1 Devotional: Chosen and Called with a Purpose

Scripture Reading: Jeremiah 1:5-8, 19 (NIV)

"Before I formed you in the womb, I knew you; before you were born I set you apart; I appointed you as a prophet to the nations."

As I reflect back on "The First Attempt," I am reminded of the truth of God's plan for my life; that plan was set in motion long before I took my first breath. "Before I formed you in the womb, I knew you." These words speak directly about the intentionality of God's calling on my life. When I look at this experience, I realize that the enemy is always trying to oppose God's purposes. He tried to stop me even when I was just five years old, but God's plans outweigh the enemy's schemes.

Before I was even conceived, God knew me. He knew the details of my life and every obstacle I would face. He knew that the enemy would come against the plan set for my life. Nevertheless, He still chose me with a specific purpose in mind and set me apart for His divine plan. Understanding that I was chosen and called with purpose gives my life direction and meaning.

Each one of us has been chosen by God for a specific purpose. You may feel insignificant at times. Maybe you feel that your life lacks worth. This scripture declares otherwise. Your life was not an accident, and you are not an afterthought! You are a deliberate creation of the Almighty, and designed to fulfill His purpose.

I Thought I Lost

As we navigate this journey of life, there will be times when we make mistakes and miss the mark. There will be moments when we feel inadequate, or unworthy. These are the times when we look to God's word for reassurance of our purpose; remembering that Jeremiah 1:5 declares that we were chosen, and God is with us.

Prayer

Dear Lord, Thank you for your grace and your love. Thank you for choosing me before I was born and setting me apart for your purpose and your will. Lord, I ask that you give me the strength and the wisdom to boldly walk out the plans that you have set before me. Let my life bring glory to Your name. In Jesus' name, Amen.

Practical Application

Jeremiah 1:5-8 declares that we are chosen, and God will rescue us in our battles. He has chosen us for purpose and regardless of the challenges, He will see us through.

Read: Read Jeremiah 1:5-8, verse 19.

Reflect: Take a moment to reflect on a time when you felt God's protection in your life. How did this experience shape your faith?

Journal: Write about your own experiences of feeling chosen and called by God. How does understanding that God knew you before you were born influence your daily life?

Pray: Spend time in prayer, asking God to reveal His purpose for your life and give you the strength to walk in it.

Angela Clemmons

I Thought I Lost

Heartfelt Reflections

Chapter 2

Undesirable Influence

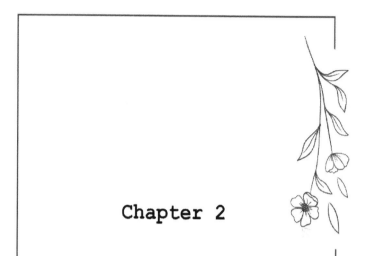

CHAPTER 2

Undesirable Influence

As a kid, my life was pretty ordinary. I did what most kids my age did: hung out with friends, rode my bike around the neighborhood, and listened to my favorite music. My life was very predictable and routine.

I lived in a typical suburban neighborhood with lots of kids my age. We would play touch football in the streets, experiencing fun and laughter as we tackled each other with playful energy. Sometimes, we would gather to learn dance routines from Michael Jackson's videos, trying to perfect the moonwalk. The most fun routine to learn was from the song "Thriller." One of my childhood passions was gymnastics. My love for gymnastics often had me spending time in the yard, tumbling, practicing cartwheels, handstands, and flips. The neighborhood was our playground, and every day brought fun times.

Music was another big part of my life. I had a box record player with a picture of Raggedy Ann on it, and I regularly played my favorite 45 rpm record, Cheryl Lynn's single "Got to Be Real." Hours were spent in my room getting lost in the melodies and lyrics of my favorite songs. I loved different genres of music, from pop to rap and gospel. Whitney Houston was my go-to. Her music inspired me in many ways, and I never grew tired of singing her songs over and over again.

My parents both worked 9-5 jobs, so I had a lot of free time after school. They worked hard to ensure the bills were paid and our needs were met, but their schedules meant that extracurricular activities were out of the question for me. I guess you could consider me a true "homegirl" because most of my time after school was spent at home. After school, my routine was simple. I'd grab a snack, usually four pieces of buttered toast with grape jelly, and settle in to do homework. Staying up to watch "The Cosby Show" would be my reward.

Despite her busy schedule and the limited time for after-school activities, my mom made sure not to neglect our faith. Growing up in a very religious home, my mom attended church with her mother and siblings every Sunday. My grandmother was deeply involved in the church community; she was a devout woman, a pillar of faith who everyone looked up to. Her days were filled with prayer, service, and a deep love for the Lord and her fellow church members.

Grandmother had an unshakeable faith that she passed down to her children. She emphasized the importance of living a life guided by the Lord. My mother inherited this strong sense of faith and commitment to the church. She believed that being spiritually grounded was important not only for herself but for her children as well. So, every Sunday, we would get up early and head to church.

It wasn't just about attending the service; it was about being part of a community that felt like an extended family. Church was more than just a Sunday obligation; it really was the glue in my upbringing. I loved singing in the choir and being part of the excitement of the church services. The choir was huge, and the best part was when we came marching into the choir stand, singing soul-stirring praises to Zion. I would rock to the right, then rock to the left, right in sync with each step. I remember the congregation clapping and singing, feeling God's presence riding on every note. And when the pastor preached, we were so inspired and uplifted by his words. My mother taught me that church was not just a place but a sanctuary where we could find strength and inspiration. These moments in church were setting a foundation and instilling values that would stay with me throughout my life.

One of my fondest memories of church is Vacation Bible School. The church van would make its way through the neighborhoods and pick up the kids, excited and ready for the promise of fun and adventure. At church, we would craft the most incredible creations, enjoy delicious snacks, and most importantly, learn about Jesus Christ. We were so excited to go to Vacation Bible School because it was a favorite event of the summer. Looking back, I realize that for our parents, it may have been a mini-vacation from parenthood, a chance to catch their breath. But for us, it was an adventure where we began to learn lessons that would develop our faith.

Going to church during my formative years made a significant mark on my life. I was introduced to the limitless love of Jesus, who sacrificed Himself to save me from my sins. At the age of 12, I was presented with an invitation that would change my life. After an awe-inspiring Sunday service, one of the youth ministers asked me if I wanted to be saved. I did not entirely understand what that meant, but there was a tug on my heart. I knew this was something I needed, so I accepted Jesus into my life. This was the beginning of my spiritual journey. From that day forward, I became aware of Jesus in my life and aspired to live according to what the Bible teaches. I tried my best to do what was "right" according to what I learned from the Bible.

My mother played a crucial role in shaping my values by taking me to church; providing me with a solid start in life. She was a loving parent and a strong role model. She instilled in me the importance of being honest and doing what was right. Life was good, and I was on the straight and narrow. However, as I transitioned into my teenage years, things began to change.

Middle school brought a significant shift in my environment and a major change in my circle of friends. This was a time of self-discovery, and not truly knowing who I was, I found myself following the crowd. Let me clarify: I was not a child out of control. I attended school every day, excelled in academics, and always heeded my parents' instructions. I was a good kid, but slowly I found myself listening to my friends a little more than my parents. The influence of peer pressure became more prevalent, and I began mimicking what I saw around me.

This is the stage where many young people start to confront identity and self-worth. For me, it was no different. My friends seemed to prioritize looking pretty, fitting in, and keeping up with the latest trends. These influences started to shape my perception of what was important. The desire to be accepted by my friends overshadowed the values I had grown up with. I remember spending more time worrying about my appearance, what clothes I wore, and how I presented myself, rather than focusing on what made me unique.

Adding to the complexity of this transitional phase was the fact that my parents were divorced. My mom had divorced my biological father when I was very young. During the summers, I would make the journey to New York to visit him. It was a time I always anticipated because it promised to be full of adventure and new experiences. My father owned a taxicab business, and one of my favorite things to do was help him maintain the cabs. My dad would let me help him change the oil in the cabs, which made me feel strong and empowered. I developed a knack for business. He told me that I had even accepted payments for cab rentals while he was out. For a brief moment, I thought I would become a mechanic. I digress.

Adapting to the different environments of my mom's home and my dad's business world in Buffalo, had its challenges. There were different dynamics and diverse influences that further contributed to my search for identity. When I visited my dad in New York, I spent a lot of time at the home of a favorite cousin. That's where all the cool kids tended to congregate. We often hung out at the field where we would break dance. One of the popular movies of that time was "Breakin'," and it had a significant influence on us. I was actually pretty good at it, and breakdancing with my friends created some of my fondest memories. Being around the cool kids and doing what they did was exciting. I wanted to belong, and following the crowd seemed like the easiest way to fit in.

One summer, while visiting my dad, I found myself spending time with some older kids at the local park. My intention wasn't to get into trouble, and I did not expect anything problematic. Did I anticipate these older kids would be smoking? Absolutely not, yet the circumstances led me to this moment: an atmosphere where these older kids were smoking marijuana. They passed the joint around, and when it reached me, I hesitated, recalling those public service announcements that shouted, "Just say no to drugs." I also thought about Jesus and the values my mother had instilled in me, knowing in my heart that this was wrong, but the enemy was working under his subtle influence.

The influence of my friends and the desire to fit in clouded my judgment. My rationale was simple; if everyone else was smoking, it must be okay. The enemy used the influence of the older kids to sway my decision to act at that moment. I did not have the courage to stand up and "Just Say NO," so I folded under the pressure, and at the tender age of 13, I took that fateful puff of marijuana.

Marijuana is often perceived as a harmless drug, but it poses significant dangers, especially for young users. Research indicates that regular marijuana use during adolescence can lead to alterations in brain function and a decrease in IQ. Marijuana use in teens is also associated with an increased risk of mental health issues such as depression and anxiety. Another serious danger is the possibility of marijuana being laced with other substances. What if that joint had been laced with some psychoactive substance? I could have lost my mind or worse, my life!

Fear kept me away from experimenting with harder drugs like cocaine or heroin. I was terrified that if I tried them once, I would immediately become addicted or die from them, so I steered clear. Marijuana wasn't something I smoked every day or even on a regular basis. It was more like an occasional experiment, but it opened the door to other questionable choices.

Navigating through these years, I often found myself in situations where my values and my desire to fit in clashed. My friends continued to influence my decisions, and I allowed their judgment to override my own. They became my compass, guiding me away from the faith-based values I had been raised with. This is a common struggle for many teenagers, and for me, it was a battle between my faith and the desire to fit in.

My mom eventually remarried, and my stepfather came into the picture. He was a great man, providing stability and security for our family. However, he also introduced a new set of rules and expectations. His perspective on discipline and structure differed from my mom's, creating tension and conflict in our home. At times, I felt misunderstood and pressured to conform to new standards. This added another layer of complexity to my journey.

Looking back, I can see how these influences shaped my decisions and steered me away from the path I had initially set out on. The choices I made during those formative years had a lasting impact on my life. They taught me valuable lessons about the power of influence, the importance of staying true to oneself, and the consequences of straying from one's values.

These experiences also underscored the importance of a strong support system. Despite the challenges, my family and faith provided a foundation that I could always return to. The lessons I learned during those years became the building blocks for my future, shaping the person I would eventually become. The journey was not without its detours, but each experience added to the richness of my story and contributed to my growth and resilience.

Angela Clemmons

Chapter 2 Devotional: The Faithfulness of God

Scripture Reading: Lamentations 3:22-25 (ESV) "The steadfast love of the Lord never ceases; His mercies never come to an end; they are new every morning; great is your faithfulness. 'The Lord is my portion,' says my soul, 'therefore I will hope in him.' The Lord is good to those who wait for him, to the soul who seeks him."

In our lives, we often encounter moments when our judgment strays far from the path we know to be right. I vividly remember one such time while visiting my father one summer. I knew I should not be in a park smoking marijuana, yet there I was. My intention was innocent, but before I knew it, I was in an atmosphere where I yielded to peer pressure.

My unwise decision could have led me down a dark path, but even in my lack of sound judgment, God's merciful hand kept me safe. When I reflect on what could have been, I am so grateful for God's mercy and grace. Despite my mistake, God did not condemn me. Psalm 103:8 (NIV) says, "The LORD is compassionate and gracious, slow to anger and abounding in love." This verse shows us that God's compassion and grace are always available to us, even when we falter.

As we navigate the journey of adulthood, the pressure to measure up and fit into societal norms doesn't diminish; it often becomes more intense. Whether in our careers, businesses, or personal lives, the weight of expectations can be overwhelming. The subtle nudges to conform can lead us to make errors in judgment or mistakes that we later regret.

Even in our challenges, God's Word offers us all the answers. Lamentations 3:22-25 reminds us of the unceasing love and faithfulness of the Lord. When we dig into the Word and stand on God's truth, we gain clarity and strength to stand against external pressures. We learn to anchor our identity in God and not in the world as we perceive it.

God's grace is overwhelming and never failing. Just as He demonstrated His mercy to me, He is a loving Father who patiently extends His mercy to you as well. No matter the mistakes we make or the times we stray from the path, we can always return to God. We can be confident in His unfailing love and faithfulness.

Prayer: Dear Lord, Thank You for Your love and mercy that never ends. Thank You for being faithful to us even when we stray from Your designated path. Help us to depend on You for guidance in every aspect of our lives. May we continually seek to follow You and place our hope in You. In Jesus' name, Amen.

Heartfelt Reflections

Welcome to this space for heartfelt reflections. Lamentations 3:22-25 reminds us that God is faithful and that His mercies are never-ending.

Read: Read Lamentations 3:22-25 and Psalm 103:8-10.

Reflect: Upon reading these scriptures, think about a time in your life when you felt surrounded by God's love. Lamentations 3 talks about new mercies each day. Write down one blessing you see in your life today.

Journal: Based on the truth of this scripture, God's mercies are never-ending. Think about the past week. How many instances has God shown you mercy? Write them down.

Rejoice: We can take comfort in knowing that past mistakes don't define us because God's love is greater than any mistake we can make. Rejoice in God's great love.

I Thought I Lost

Chapter 3

Innocence Lost

CHAPTER 3

Innocence Lost

As I transitioned into high school, the desire to fit in escalated to a new level. The pressures to be accepted by peers became more intense, often leading young people to conform to social standards that didn't quite align with the principles by which they were raised. High school is a time when the pursuit of identity becomes even more pronounced, and the stakes feel higher. This pursuit of fitting in can be constructive on one hand but destructive on another.

During high school, I experienced both the positive and negative aspects of peer pressure. While striving to be accepted, I sometimes found myself compromising on values that were important to me. I had almost forgotten some of these experiences, as they were tucked neatly away in the depths of my memory, only to resurface as I started the journey of writing. It's incredible how some events are stored in the recesses of our minds, seemingly insignificant, because we choose not to remember them.

The excitement and innocence of stepping into a completely new environment, full of promise and potential, were quickly overshadowed by the harsh realities of high school. I found myself back at square one. Entering high school, I was eager to make friends and find my place. This was especially significant to me because I had felt invisible in middle school. I did not want to go into high school being that same invisible person. The desire to fit in began to shape my decisions and actions in ways that I had not anticipated. I yearned to be popular and to be "in" with the crowd.

One of the ways I sought friends was through extracurricular activities. My mother had encouraged me to participate in gymnastics during my childhood, and it was a sport where I excelled. Because of my tumbling skills, I took a shot at auditioning for the cheerleading team, and I was super excited when I made the cut! Joining the cheerleading squad was like stepping immediately into the spotlight.

Now, being a part of the sports community opened a whole new world to me. It was an automatic entrance to the world of popularity! Instantly, I was surrounded by newfound friends, and my social life blossomed in ways I had only dreamed of. Suddenly, I was no longer invisible; I was part of the "in crowd," most would say. Being a cheerleader brought a sense of immediate recognition; everyone knew our names.

I had gained access to the coveted social circle of high school teens. However, this new level of popularity came with the pressure to "fit in" and to adhere and conform to the behaviors of my friends. In these social circles, my peers were preoccupied with looking cute, party invitations, how cute the boys were, and pursuing romantic relationships. And yes, teens were even talking about the topic of sex! As a 14-year-old freshman in high school, I was not prepared for this.

Let me inform you that sex was not a topic of discussion in my home as I was growing up. Sex was a taboo subject. Not a very comfortable discussion for most parents to have with their children, would you agree? What I remember about the sex talk is the question of whether I wanted to take the pill. Absolutely not! I assured my mother that I wasn't going to need birth control pills. Although there were lots of kids out there having sex, I was not one of them!

The strong message from my church, however, was the importance of remaining pure until marriage. According to the Bible, sex before marriage is a sin. Scripture reminds us in 1 Thessalonians 4:3-4, "For this is the will of God, your sanctification: that you abstain from fornication; that each one of you know how to control his own body in holiness and honor." As a new believer, I didn't fully understand the consequences of pre-marital sex, and there wasn't an extensive explanation for the "why." Nevertheless, I was committed to doing the right thing, so I listened and attempted to live by what I was taught.

However, the devil knew the consequences and used various tactics to challenge my commitment to chastity. This was part of his plan to destroy my destiny and purpose. Many of my friends and peers did not share my convictions about sex before marriage. They created an image of sex as something romantic. They made it sound delicious, as if sex was something that I should crave.

The scenario was similar to the time in Genesis 3 when the serpent deceived Eve into eating the fruit of the tree. Genesis 3:1 describes the serpent (the devil) as crafty. "You will not die," the serpent told Eve in verse 5. No, Eve didn't die, but innocence was destroyed. The enemy used the influence of my friends to fill my mind with stories of sensuality as being something that was the norm. At the age of 14, I was quite innocent and impressionable. "It's cool," they said, "everyone is doing it." I trusted their words.

I had no intention of looking for someone to have sex with, but as a freshman, being considered "fresh meat" meant the guys came looking. Promiscuity was never my path, and I was not overly infatuated with boys. However, the constant pressure from my friends to just try it eventually wore me down. One day after a school game, in a moment of vulnerability, my innocence was surrendered to a boy who wasn't even considered a boyfriend! Virginity was lost, leaving me in disbelief. I asked myself, "How did this happen to a 'good' girl like me?" Within just a few minutes, the damage was done and could not be reversed.

Initially, there was a naive belief that this experience would bring some sense of satisfaction. Strangely, excitement was felt as the story was shared with my friends, as if having sex for the first time was a significant achievement. Yet, the emotional aftermath that followed was unexpected and overwhelming. There was immediate regret, which reminded me of the biblical story of Eve eating the forbidden fruit, then realizing she was naked! Feelings of nakedness and shame filled my mind, with absolutely no positive emotions about this situation.

Outwardly, I maintained a facade, portraying to my friends that everything was fine, and that being "cool" was all that mattered. Yet inside, I agonized because this was far from the person I aspired to be. The weight of the irreversible decision was heavy, and there was no way to undo what had been done.

Embarrassment prevented me from confiding in my mother because I feared her disappointment, especially after assuring her that being with a boy was not in my plans. This action has now made me a liar, casting doubts on how she could ever trust me again.

Sharing this situation with someone from church was not an option either, as the teachings on abstaining from sex before marriage were clear. I dreaded the thought of their judgment, making this an impossible conversation to have.

The enemy set a sex trap, and I fell right into it. That's what the enemy does. He is a deceiver and tricks us into thinking we are missing out on something important. I was duped into giving up something that was so valuable and irretrievable. He then used this situation to dump feelings of emptiness and impurity on me. He planted the notion that I was "used goods," intensifying my sense of loss and regret.

Reflecting on the teaching in John 10, which talks about the adversary's intent to steal, kill, and destroy, it was so evident how close I came to facing major consequences, such as becoming pregnant the first time I had sex, or contracting a lifelong incurable disease! Teens don't generally consider these types of consequences before making decisions. This had to be one of the biggest mistakes of my youth. The Bible admonishes us to present our bodies as living sacrifices and to be holy. I had certainly missed the mark, but despite it all, God showed me grace.

I Thought I Lost

Weighed down by feelings of shame and dirtiness, I often felt unworthy and thought low of myself. These emotions were heavy, making it difficult to see my worth. However, even in the depths of my shame and guilt, I still heard a voice in my heart reminding me of God's unconditional love. The teachings from church emphasized that his forgiveness was available to me. 1 John 1:9 clearly states: "If we confess our sins, he is faithful and just and will forgive us our sins and purify us from all unrighteousness." Internalizing this truth helped me to understand his forgiveness and to overcome my feelings of shame and impurity.

This experience taught me that following others can lead to poor decisions. I learned that it is far better to be a leader than a follower and that I am much stronger than I had given myself credit for. It is truly amazing how God's great mercy shielded me from the repercussions of teen pregnancy and venereal disease. Not only did He remove my shame, but He also provided me with an opportunity to learn and grow from what I considered a mistake. God's love is bigger than any mistake, and His grace allowed me to move forward with greater wisdom and resilience.

During this time, I also learned the importance of prayer and seeking God for myself. I realized that prayers don't have to be extravagant or perfect; God hears us regardless of how simple or complex our words might be. According to 1 John 5:14, "This is the confidence we have in approaching God: that if we ask anything according to His will, He hears us." This gave me the strength to pray for myself and trust that God was listening.

Angela Clemmons

As I continued to grow in faith, I realized the importance of knowing scriptures that talk about forgiveness and overcoming. Verses like 1 John 1:9, "If we confess our sins, He is faithful and just and will forgive us our sins and purify us from all unrighteousness," and Philippians 4:13, "I can do all things through Christ who strengthens me." These verses became my go-to's to help me stay strong by emphasizing the truth that God's forgiveness is always available and that we can overcome any challenge with His help.

It is important to recognize that if you've made mistakes in your own life, you have the capacity to move beyond them. Internalize these truths and understand that through His forgiveness, we are equipped to continue our journey toward our destined purpose. By standing on the power of prayer and the wisdom found in God's word, we can find the strength to overcome our past and move forward with confidence.

Chapter 3 Devotional: God's Forgiveness and Forgetfulness

Scripture for Reflection:

"If we confess our sins, he is faithful and just and will forgive us our sins and purify us from all unrighteousness." — 1 John 1:9 (NIV)

As we transition into new chapters of our lives, the desire to fit in and be accepted can often lead us to make decisions that don't align with our values. High school, for instance, is a time when the pursuit of identity feels crucial, and the pressures of peer acceptance can be intense. I experienced this firsthand when my eagerness to fit in led me to compromise on my principles. Despite my upbringing and commitment to remain pure until marriage, I eventually succumbed to the pressure. In a moment of vulnerability, I lost my virginity to a boy who wasn't my boyfriend.

This caused me regret, shame, and a sense of unworthiness. I felt as if I had strayed far from who I wanted to be, and the weight of my mistake was heavy. However, it was during this low point that I remembered the promise of 1 John 1:9 — that if we confess our sins, God is faithful and just to forgive us and purify us from all unrighteousness.

God's forgiveness is profound and complete. When we confess our mistakes to Him, He not only forgives us but also throws our sins into a sea of forgetfulness, saying "no fishing." This means we don't have to dwell on our past mistakes once we give them to God. His grace allows us to move forward with a clean slate, free from the burdens of guilt and shame.

This experience taught me that God's love and mercy are greater than any mistake we can make. I learned the importance of prayer and seeking God's guidance. Prayers don't need to be elaborate; God hears us regardless of how simple our words are. This understanding gave me the strength to pray and trust that God was listening, offering me forgiveness and a chance to start new.

Prayer: Heavenly Father, thank You for unending love and forgiveness. Help us to remember that when we confess our sins, You are faithful and just to forgive us and purify us from all unrighteousness. Give us the strength to let go of our past mistakes and to move forward with confidence, knowing that You have thrown our sins into a sea of forgetfulness. In Jesus' name, Amen.

Heartfelt Reflections

Take a moment to look within yourself. Is there something you need to give to God? Confess it, and trust that He is faithful to forgive you. Release your past mistakes and step confidently into the future, knowing that God's grace covers you.

Read: Read 1 John 1:9 and Ephesians 3:12. Take a moment to confess any sins or mistakes to God. Trust in His promise to forgive and purify you.

Reflect: Remember that God throws your sins into a sea of forgetfulness, so let go of any lingering guilt. Approach God with confidence in prayer. Ephesians 3:12 reminds us that "In him and through faith in him we may approach God with freedom and confidence." Trust that He hears you and is ready to guide you through any challenges.

Journal: How will you apply the truths of God's forgiveness and forgetfulness to your life today? Write down your reflections and steps you will take to embrace a fresh start, free from the burdens of the past?

Rejoice: Thank God for a fresh start. Understand that through God's grace, you are given a fresh start. Embrace this new beginning with the knowledge that you are loved and forgiven, and move forward with greater wisdom and resilience.

I Thought I Lost

Chapter 4

New Influence

CHAPTER 4
New Influence

Life is a journey that does not stop because of the mistakes we make. You can grow from them when you choose to learn from them. We all have the capacity to use those very mistakes as stepping stones to our next level of growth. I learned a profound lesson about the power of choice when it comes to relationships.

One pivotal choice was deciding not to engage in sexual relationships with teenage boys. When you choose not to engage in sexual relationships with teenage boys, they lose interest fast. I welcomed this change because it allowed me to focus on nurturing my developing relationship with God. I gained a new perspective on intimacy, coming to see my body as a sacred offering to God, a concept rooted in Romans 8, verses 1 and 2. This scripture emphasizes living according to the Spirit rather than the flesh, and it transformed how I viewed my body and my worth.

This shift in my perspective extended beyond intimacy. I began to understand how the company we keep makes a significant impact on the decisions we make. Surrounding myself with friends who shared my values and beliefs became essential. It became crystal clear that changes in my peer circles were necessary to successfully navigate life, especially during these influential years of high school.

Angela Clemmons

Choosing to stand apart from the crowd became a pivotal lesson in my journey. In a culture that constantly pressures us to conform, I discovered the strength in embracing my individuality. The crowd can often lead us down paths that diverge from our values and God's plan for us. This realization reinforced my commitment to staying true to my beliefs, even when it meant walking alone. However, despite recognizing the importance of standing firm on my own convictions, I still needed positive role models outside of my teachers at school.

Getting my confidence back meant diving into my studies and focusing on getting back on track. Making my schoolwork a priority and setting goals helped me regain a sense of purpose and direction. I immersed myself in my studies, actively participating in class, and seeking additional help from teachers when needed. These efforts were not only about improving my grades but also about rediscovering my passion for learning and developing a strong work ethic.

As I worked hard to improve myself, I felt a desire for something more than just academic achievement. I could not put my finger on it, but I sensed that there was a greater purpose waiting to be discovered. That "more" became clear upon seeing a girl named Sylvia gliding down the hall with a highly decorated, green uniform and a burgundy beret. She was smart, beautiful, and confident. Sylvia was a leader, and I admired her tremendously. Her unique swag sparked a realization: a desire for leadership was being birthed within me. Sylvia became a role model, exactly what was needed to inspire me to strive for excellence beyond the classroom.

Curiosity quickly took over, compelling me to seek a deeper understanding of what gave her this strength and confidence to excel as a teen. The answer was the Junior Reserve Officers' Training Corps, better known as JROTC. Intrigued by the discipline, camaraderie, and opportunities for leadership that JROTC offered, I decided to join. This was the next step in my growth. The program challenged me in new ways, teaching me the importance of teamwork, responsibility, and perseverance. Through JROTC, I began to develop the same poise and self-assurance that had initially drawn me to Sylvia, laying a foundation for the leadership qualities that would shape my future.

Joining JROTC provided the structure and discipline that would be essential for my growth as a leader. This program offered a community that valued integrity, perseverance, and excellence. Herein lay the positive influences that reinforced the importance of choosing the right path, even if it meant standing apart from the crowd. JROTC promoted the development of leadership skills and the importance of character, self-discipline, respect, and teamwork. Those were just the things that I needed.

I excelled in the JROTC program and even went on to become the Military Ball Queen! This achievement was a significant milestone, not just for the title, but for what it represented personally. Becoming the Military Ball Queen symbolized my growth, confidence, and the respect I had earned from my fellow classmates and teachers. This honor reflected my hard work and dedication to the program. Being recognized encouraged me to continue striving for greater things.

Angela Clemmons

Initially, I saw ROTC as an amazing class that offered me incredible opportunities. However, God was using this class to prepare me for the next chapter in my life. Reflecting on this, Isaiah chapter 55:8-9 comes to mind: "For my thoughts are not your thoughts, neither are your ways my ways," declares the LORD. "As the heavens are higher than the earth, so are my ways higher than your ways and my thoughts than your thoughts."

Undoubtedly, God's plan was unfolding in ways I could not have predicted. JROTC was not just about learning military drills or wearing a uniform; it was about becoming a stronger, better version of myself. It helped me grow in leadership and develop resilience. I was no longer the girl trying to fit in with the crowd. I gained confidence and a sense of purpose. JROTC taught me how to be strong and lead, transforming me from someone who sought to blend in, into someone who sought to stand out and inspire others.

JROTC instilled in me the desire to "be all that I could be." So, when the opportunity arose to earn money for college and enter the military with rank, I acted on it and joined the Army Reserves. It turns out that JROTC was the right circle of influence for me, shaping my future in ways I had not have imagined. The program laid a foundation of discipline and leadership that would carry me through life's challenges; continually pushing me towards excellence and reminding me of the importance of integrity and perseverance.

A vital lesson I learned during this time was that I was capable of more than I had ever imagined. Each challenge I overcame and each goal achieved reinforced my belief in myself and my commitment to excellence. Naturally, joining the Army Reserves felt like the next logical step after my time in JROTC.

Feeling a deep sense of pride about my decision to join the Army Reserves, I was excited to continue this journey. My parents were proud of me, and I felt honored to follow in the footsteps of many of my uncles who had served in the military. This decision was highly esteemed by my family, especially since one of my uncles had made the ultimate sacrifice, dying in combat. Their legacy filled me with a profound respect for the path I had chosen.

Training Produces Growth

Upon graduating high school, my summer did not begin like most kids. I had a few weeks' break before preparing for Basic Training, which was the next level on my life journey. The anticipation was a mix of excitement and nerves, knowing that I was about to face a rigorous challenge. Soon, I found myself shipped off to Fort Jackson, South Carolina, for eight weeks of Basic Training, also known as boot camp.

Arriving in the desert-like heat of June, I quickly realized that this would be an entirely new challenge compared to JROTC. The intensity of the summer heat was unyielding and the rigors of Basic Training demanded a level of toughness and determination I had yet to experience. This transition was the beginning of the next chapter of my life, where the lessons and skills from JROTC would be put to the ultimate test in a real-world environment.

Angela Clemmons

Basic Training was a huge step up from the JROTC program I had excelled in during high school. The physical challenges were much more demanding. I was not used to 5 a.m. wake-up calls. Those early mornings were tough, but they built my endurance and taught me the importance of teamwork. Physical training was far more intense than anything I had done in JROTC. Another aspect of boot camp, kitchen duty, reinforced the importance of responsibility and cooperation. Working in the mess hall required a strong work ethic and collaboration to feed all the soldiers, and I made sure I excelled at that task!

Each challenge at Basic Training reinforced my belief in myself, proving that I was capable of achieving even more. However, being away from home for the first time was both exciting and intimidating. In the initial weeks of training, I struggled with homesickness, longing for the comforts of home and my mother's reassuring hugs. It was in these challenging moments that bonds formed with fellow soldiers would be invaluable. These comrades were a support system that helped me navigate and endure the trials we faced.

Throughout this new path on my journey, I witnessed God's hand at work. What started out as a high school elective turned into a path that would develop my character, provide for my education, and open doors to my future that I could not have created for myself. God's ways are truly higher than ours, and His plans for us often reveal themselves in ways we do not expect.

Basic training was completed, my initiation into the Armed Forces. As I embarked on the next phase of my journey—Advanced

Individual Training—here, I would acquire the specialized skills necessary for my role in the Army, continuing to build upon the foundation laid by JROTC and Basic Training.

In Basic, I had grasped the fundamentals of military life. The physical training was intense, pushing me to limits I hadn't known I could reach. I left home a slim young lady weighing 120 pounds, but by the completion of Basic, I had transformed into a stronger version of myself, now weighing 140 pounds, having gained significant muscle. This rigorous training not only enhanced my physical strength and stamina but also increased my mental toughness and sharpened my critical thinking skills.

Now, it was time to acquire the specialized training and skills necessary for my role as a Materiel Control and Accounting Specialist, MOS 76P in the Army. I was headed to Fort Lee, VA, a place where I would dive deep into learning the intricacies of my job assignment. Here, I would learn to manage and account for military supplies, ensuring that every piece of equipment was tracked and maintained efficiently. The responsibility was immense, but I felt ready to take it on.

The transition from Basic Training to Advanced Individual Training marked a significant milestone. Each new challenge was an opportunity to build upon the foundation I had laid during Basic Training. The discipline, tenacity, and skills I had developed would now be tested and refined even further.

As I reflected on the journey that had brought me to Fort Lee, I realized how much I had grown. The new influences and experiences had shaped me into a whole new person, a young woman still on the path toward discovering her purpose. At Fort Lee, I would be surrounded by others who, like me, were eager to advance their capabilities and serve our country with excellence. I embraced the challenges ahead, prepared to excel as a proficient Materiel Control and Accounting Specialist, ready to contribute to the Army's mission.

In the Fall of 1990, I successfully completed my AIT (Advanced Individual Training) and proudly earned the title of 76P, Materiel Control and Accounting Specialist. God's guiding hand had been evident throughout every trial and triumph. The journey toward purpose continues.

Chapter 4 Devotional: New Influences, New Circles

Scripture for Reflection:

"Walk with the wise and become wise, for a companion of fools suffers harm." — Proverbs 13:20 (NIV)

Life is a journey where the influences we allow into our lives significantly shape who we become. The company we keep can either uplift us or lead us astray. Proverbs 13:20 reminds us that walking with the wise leads to wisdom, while associating with fools brings harm.

During my high school years, I realized the importance of surrounding myself with positive influences and mentors. Changing my peer circles became necessary for my personal growth and to navigate life successfully. Standing apart from the crowd and embracing my individuality strengthened my commitment to stay true to my beliefs, even when it meant walking alone.

One significant milestone was joining the Junior Reserve Officers' Training Corps (JROTC). This program provided structure, discipline, and a sense of community. It helped me to surround myself with people who had strong values, encouraging me to think bigger and aspire for more. Through JROTC, I developed leadership qualities that shaped my future, transforming me into someone striving to inspire others.

Positive mentors and connections play a crucial role in our development and personal evolution. They guide us, encourage us, and help us recognize the potential within ourselves. God, in His wisdom, will align us with the right people to advance our purpose. All we need to do is seek them out!

Prayer: Heavenly Father, Thank You for Your guidance and for placing the right influences in our lives. Help us make wise choices in our relationships and surround ourselves with people who uplift and inspire us. Give us the strength to stand firm in our values and follow the path You have set before us. In Jesus' name, Amen.

Heartfelt Reflection: Consider the role of new influences and circles in your life. Are there areas where you need to seek out positive role models or make changes to your social environment? Reflect on how God might be guiding you through these new connections.

Read: Read Proverbs 13:20, 1 Corinthians 15:33, Proverbs 27:17, Proverbs 14:7

Reflect: Reflect on your current social circles. Are the people around you uplifting and encouraging you to grow and excel? Are they leading you to be more like God? If not, seek out new influences that align with your values.Engage in activities and communities that challenge you to grow and strive for excellence. Be yourself. Stand firm in your beliefs, even if it means standing alone. Trust that God's plan for you is unique.

Journal: Based on these scriptures, how will you apply the truths of God's guidance and the importance of new influences to your life today? Write down your reflections and the steps you will take to champion positive changes and growth.

Rejoice: Thank God in advance for sending the right social connections and mentors who will sharpen your iron. Rejoice in the revelation of God's word, which brings transformation and progress, elevating you to new heights. Celebrate the positive changes and growth you are experiencing as you align yourself with His purpose and guidance

Chapter 5

War Did not Stop Me

I Thought I Lost

CHAPTER 5
War Did Not Stop Me

Returning home as a transformed individual and now a soldier, I began my journey with the rank of Private First Class, earned through JROTC training in high school. Joining the 844th Engineering Battalion in Knoxville, TN, I was eager to serve with dedication and apply my newly acquired skills in the local Reserve unit. Everything seemed promising stateside, but unbeknownst to many, a major crisis was unfolding on the other side of the world.

As tensions over oil production and debt disputes between Iraq and Kuwait reached a boiling point, the unthinkable happened: Saddam Hussein invaded Kuwait. This marked the first major foreign crisis for the United States since the Cold War. In a swift response, the U.S. deployed a significant number of soldiers to the region to deter further aggression and protect Saudi Arabia. The emerging conflict dominated conversations around our military motor pool in my reserve unit as we braced for the possibility of going to war.

During my first weekend drill after completing AIT, the whispers about the impending conflict became impossible to ignore. Rumors were plentiful that our unit would be deployed, and I was stunned. Fresh out of Basic and AIT training, I hadn't imagined that I'd be heading to war so soon. Operation Desert Shield involved the deployment of hundreds of thousands of American troops and allied forces, and it wasn't long before our Reserve unit, the 844th Engineering Battalion, was called up as well.

At just 18 years old, fresh out of high school, Desert Storm had not been on my radar. My plans had included college, getting an education, and having some fun. I had signed up to serve one weekend per month and two weeks per year. This was not what I expected in any shape or form. The reality of war hit hard, transforming my youthful optimism into a sobering readiness for the unknown challenges ahead.

As the winter of 1990 approached, my reserve unit was mobilized at Fort Bragg, NC, in preparation for our overseas deployment to Saudi Arabia. The atmosphere at Fort Bragg was a mix of urgency and meticulous planning. We were thrown into an intense routine designed to get us ready for the realities of active duty. There were endless drills, equipment checks, and immunizations! Each day, we trained harder and pushed our limits, both physically and mentally.

Being on my own in active duty military was a completely different experience. Gone were the comforts of home and the familiarity of reserve duty. Every morning started with rigorous physical training sessions that tested our endurance and strength. I was so green, fresh out of basic training. One morning, as I rushed to make formation on time, I arrived with my Kevlar helmet on backward! Something we laugh about to this day is that I was so "new" they called me "Private Benjamin." You will have to read between the lines on that! After PT, we moved on to tactical training, learning how to navigate the desert we would soon face. Countless hours were spent in study and preparation for the trek we would soon take to the Middle East.

Living as a soldier on active duty was a huge contrast to my previous life. I felt a mix of emotions – pride in serving my country, anxiety about the upcoming deployment, and a sobering realization of the seriousness of our mission.

It was the first time that I would journey this far from home, and I felt like I had to become an adult overnight. I was going to war, over 7,000 miles away from everything familiar. Was I afraid? Absolutely! I was terrified! We were heading into a foreign country where the threat of being shot at, injured, or killed loomed over us.

Despite the challenges, this period at Fort Bragg was crucial in transforming us from reservists into a cohesive, battle-ready unit. Amid all the new changes and training, I had a deep, confident feeling that God was still leading me and had me taken care of. This faith provided me with a sense of peace and strength, knowing I wasn't alone on this journey.

Life in Saudi - Desert Storm

After months of rigorous training, our deployment to Saudi Arabia introduced a new set of challenges. Transitioning from the structured environment of the barracks at Fort Bragg to the unpredictable reality of war required immediate adaptation. In January 1991, after 18 hours in the air, we arrived in Saudi Arabia. The anticipation of involvement in a conflict had now become a reality.

There was the ever-present danger of biological and chemical warfare, extreme temperatures, and intense psychological stress. The comforts of home and home-cooked meals were a distant memory. My warm bed and the luxury of hot running water for showers were gone. I had also left behind my boyfriend—my first love. Everything normal had changed.

All of this was exchanged for a tent in the Saudi Arabian desert, cold showers, and a platoon of soldiers with whom I would spend the next 7 months of my life. Although I had completed months of physical and classroom training, including learning to use gas masks, weapons, and ammunition, nothing could truly prepare me for the unknown challenges ahead. Despite the fear, I pressed on, relying on God to get me back home.

One of the biggest challenges I faced being on my own was not being able to contact my mother. I couldn't just pick up the phone and call her for advice or pop by her bedroom for a warm hug. There was no kitchen to walk into and grab my favorite meal. Instead, most of our meals came in thick brown plastic packages called MREs. These meals tasted nothing like my mom's home cooking, but they did provide the necessary nutrition. My two favorite MREs were Chicken Cacciatore and Chicken à la King. We would heat these meals by placing them in metal bowls of boiling water atop kerosene heaters inside our tents.

One good thing about our unit was that we had KPs, also known as kitchen police, who could really cook. While they didn't prepare meals for us every day, occasionally, we would enjoy a nice soulful meal, providing a brief but much-needed taste of home during these harsh conditions.

I Thought I Lost

Although I was without the comfort of home and my mother's hugs, she did send hugs in a box, called care packages. The care packages included toiletries, snacks, and one of the soldiers' all-time favorites—Nissin Cup noodles. When those packages arrived, I was overwhelmed with gratitude, as I received a little taste of home.

This deployment matured me daily. Though I managed the day-to-day, I missed home deeply. I missed my friends and the boyfriend who never wrote. Although I was surrounded by soldiers, loneliness often crept in. I longed for my friends, family, work, and the smell of Krystal burgers, my favorite restaurant. While mail day excited most soldiers, it was my father's letters I eagerly awaited. His words of love and pride were a highlight, offering brief escapes from the harsh reality of war.

Living in a tent in the desert for six months was far from easy, but God's presence was always felt. Despite the challenges, His promise in Deuteronomy 31:6, 8—that He would never fail or abandon—was a constant source of strength.

Daily tasks were diligently completed, often extending beyond the training received in military school. Unexpected duties frequently arose, including sanitation duty, which involved maintaining the notorious burn pits. These pits required burning bathroom waste in huge barrels, undoubtedly one of the most unpleasant tasks I encountered.

Pulling watch guard duty was another essential responsibility, requiring staying awake overnight and armed to secure the post. This duty was always performed with another soldier, creating a bond of trust as our lives depended on each other. Through many sleepless nights standing guard together, a deep camaraderie developed as well as mutual reliance and support.

During this deployment, my comrades became family in the absence of my own. We shared meals, bunked together, and faced the daily grind side by side. Occasionally, we found moments to relax and play. I learned to play chess and became quite good at Spades! Through these experiences, many of us forged lifelong connections and found much-needed reprieve from the challenges we faced.

Amidst the hardships and unexpected duties, a newfound strength and tenacity emerged. Each challenge faced and every bond formed reassured me of my faith and helped me realize that I was not alone. Being deployed during this war deepened my gratitude and built my trust in God's protection and guidance that never changes. Deep in my heart, it was clear that God was watching over me. Psalms 91 protection surrounded me, especially Verse 7: "A thousand shall fall at thy side, and ten thousand at thy right hand; But it shall not come nigh thee."

The Persian Gulf War lasted nearly seven months from the initial invasion of Kuwait by Iraq. During those seven months, a transformation took place, turning a young woman into someone much stronger than before leaving home. Living in the desert, surrounded by the constant threat of danger, often led to reflections on purpose and faith. Each challenge reinforced a belief in God's plan, teaching trust in His protection even when the future seemed uncertain. Although danger was all around, no harm came because life is part of His divine plan.

I Thought I Lost

You may look back over your life and recall a time when you faced perilous circumstances. Things didn't turn out according to your plans, yet here you are today. God protected you because He has a plan for your life. This war was far from anything I could have envisioned, but the truth is that God's plans surpass our own every day. He is ultimately in control of our lives, and for me, there was undoubtedly more ahead.

Angela Clemmons

Chapter 5 Devotional: Trusting God's Protection

Scripture Reading:

Deuteronomy 31:6, 8 (NIV) "Be strong and courageous. Do not be afraid or terrified because of them, for the Lord your God goes with you; he will never leave you nor forsake you."

Psalm 91:1, 2, 4 (NIV) "Whoever dwells in the shelter of the Most High will rest in the shadow of the Almighty. I will say of the Lord, 'He is my refuge and my fortress, my God, in whom I trust.' He will cover you with his feathers, and under his wings you will find refuge; his faithfulness will be your shield and rampart."

Imagine the sudden uprooting, the unexpected call to duty when you are in the process of beginning your life. Like many unexpected challenges we face, this deployment to Saudi Arabia during Desert Storm was unimaginable. As we reflect on Chapter 5 of this journey, we encounter a powerful truth: God's faithfulness endures through the uncertainties of life.

In those initial days of deployment, surrounded by fear and unpredictability, I clung to God's promise of protection. Despite the distance from loved ones, the harsh conditions, and the imminent danger, His presence brought a peace that I held tight to. Spending time in the secret place, praying to God, I found not just physical protection but also a deep assurance that His plans for me were secure.

When our plans are disrupted, when the future seems unpredictable, it's easy to feel overwhelmed. Yet, in those moments,

God's promise remains steadfast: He will never leave us nor forsake us. Just as He guided through the turmoil of war in the Persian Gulf, He will continue to guide us through every storm of life.

Prayer: Lord, Your promises are our foundation in times when life does not make sense. Thank You for giving us the privilege of entering your secret place; the place of your presence and protection. Help us to trust in Your plan, knowing that Your peace will guard our hearts and minds. May we continually dwell securely in Your shelter, finding refuge under Your wings. In Jesus' name,

Heartfelt Reflection: When you become overwhelmed, remember, God invites you to call on Him. He promises to answer and be with you in times of trouble. Psalm 91 is filled with assurances of His protection because He loves us. When you feel afraid, it's important to stand on God's promises. How often do we face situations that seem beyond our control? It's in those moments that we must lean into God's promises. Whether it's navigating a crisis, facing seemingly insurmountable challenges, or simply dealing with unexpected changes, meditate on Psalm 91, knowing that God is already there, working out His perfect plan.

Read: Read Psalm 91 slowly and attentively.

Reflect: Reflect on specific times when you felt God's guiding hand or experienced His peace during turmoil. Explore how Psalm 91 and other promises of God's protection resonate with your current challenges or anxieties. How has God's presence and faithfulness been evident in moments of uncertainty or challenge in your life?

Journal: Consider moments when life took an unexpected turn. How did these experiences shape your faith and perspective on God's purpose for your life? After reading Psalm 91, how does knowing the truth of God's faithfulness affect your outlook now? What will you do differently when you feel anxious and encounter complex situations?

Rejoice: Thank God in advance for sending the right social connections and mentors who will sharpen your iron. Rejoice in the revelation of God's word, which brings transformation and progress, elevating you to new heights. Celebrate the positive changes and growth you are experiencing as you align yourself with His purpose and guidance.

I Thought I Lost

Chapter 6

Through the Storm

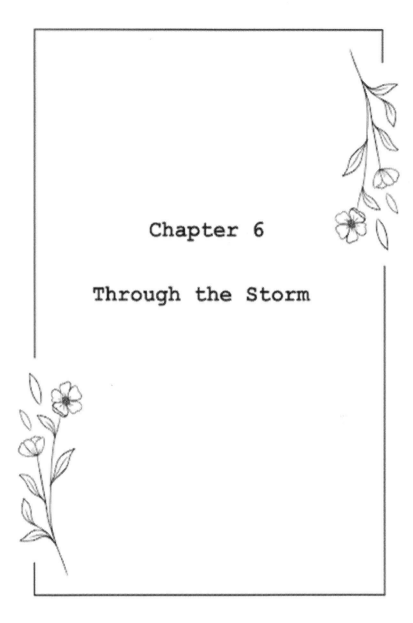

Angela Clemmons

CHAPTER 6
Through the Storm

It was July of 1991. The Gulf War had ended, and our unit returned to Knoxville, TN. We were celebrated as heroes, yet the true transformation was internal. I had departed as a young girl but returned home as an adult, forever changed by the experience of war.

In the midst of our homecoming celebrations, I felt a mix of triumph and disorientation. The war had changed me, both inside and out. It had brought me love, but it had also thrown me off course, challenging my sense of identity and purpose. This chapter of my life was not just about returning from war—it was about finding my way back to myself and discovering God's plan amidst everything swirling around me.

During our tour in Saudi Arabia, I met the young man who would become my husband. He was in the same reserve unit, and our initial encounter was less than promising. At first, he seemed like the most arrogant person I had ever met—I couldn't stand him! Yet, as time went on, we quickly became good friends. He became like a brother to me, a familiar face in an unfamiliar land.

The funny thing about war is that when you are away from family and loved ones, you cling to those who are near. In the midst of the desert, surrounded by the uncertainties of battle, we found comfort in

I Thought I Lost

each other's presence. I didn't see it coming, but we fell in love amidst the sands of Saudi Arabia. Interestingly, despite living only a block away from each other, it took a war almost 8,000 miles away to bring us together.

We survived the war. Exhale. At 19 years old, as I prepared for college, a significant life change took place with the discovery of a first pregnancy. Being unmarried and pregnant was far from what I had imagined for myself. As a Christian, knowing what the Scriptures said about fornication, my growing belly became a source of shame. I feared judgment from churchgoers.

Initially, the weight of letting God down felt heavy. Sinning against Him was wrong, and I knew better. I was a novice in my relationship with Christ and overlooked the fact that my then-fiancé was unsaved. My shame stemmed from the perceived judgment of others. I had not yet realized that others' opinions were insignificant compared to God's view of me.

There were many thoughts that filled my mind as I carried this child. Would I have to quit college? What if my fiancé decided to leave because we were unmarried? Would God turn His back on me because of my sin? The worries seemed endless.

During this period, I gained a deeper understanding of God's character and who He really is. When I confided in my father about my pregnancy, I expected extreme disappointment. However, my father encouraged me by sharing Proverbs 3:5-6: "Trust in the Lord with all your heart and lean not on your own understanding; in all your ways submit to Him, and He will make your paths straight." My father reassured me of his love and lack of condemnation. It became clear that God did not condemn me either. I could ask for forgiveness, and God would throw my sins into the depths of the sea. Walking in God's forgiveness allowed me to hold my head high.

The weight of my situation still felt heavy at times. I struggled with the fear of an uncertain future and the shame of my perceived failures. Yet, in those quiet moments, when the world seemed judgmental and I felt most alone, the depth of God's grace became evident. His love is not conditional upon our perfection but is a promise to guide us through our darkest valleys.

In the midst of my turmoil, I found comfort in prayer and Scripture, clinging to verses that spoke of God's unending mercy and forgiveness. Slowly, it became clear that His plan for me was far greater than my mistakes. It was a journey of faith, learning to see myself through God's eyes rather than through the lens of people who judged me.

With this new revelation of God's character, I walked in the reassurance of His love for me. The stares no longer had power over me. As my belly grew, so did my faith. Each day was a step towards embracing my identity in Christ, understanding that His love for me was unending. I was not defined by my past but by His promises for my future.

My daughter was born in the spring of 1992. Life now, had taken on new meaning. No longer was I responsible just for myself; a new purpose had emerged—to care for my precious baby. Embracing my identity as a mother, everything shifted. The moment I held my daughter for the first time, an overwhelming sense of love washed over me. It was an emotion so profound, a feeling of love that's unexplainable, yet unmistakable. This new love gave me a deeper understanding of God's love for His children. Just as I loved my daughter unconditionally, I realized the depth of God's love for me.

The following year, in 1993, marriage brought further changes, followed swiftly by the birth of my second child. At just 21 years old, with two children and a new marriage, my inexperience as a mother and wife was challenging. Determined to be the best mother and wife possible, I clung to the wisdom imparted by my Grandmother, Irene. Her parting words after every phone conversation, "Be a good little wife, and a good little mother," rang in my heart. Those words became a guide for me, a constant reminder of the aspiration to live up to her loving instructions.

This new chapter of life would lead to profound growth. It was a time to learn, to lean into God's unchanging hand for support, and to embrace the roles of wife and mother with grace and determination.

At 23 years old, life seemed to be unfolding beautifully. As a young wife and mother of two, I hadn't finished college yet, but God's hand was evident in our lives. He opened doors, providing good jobs for both me and my husband, and we thrived as a family. We walked by faith. On Sundays, we attended church and participated actively in ministry. I sang in the choir, and together, my husband and I dedicated our time to the Children's church. Our two daughters were our pride and joy, but deep within me, there was a yearning for a son. At 24, we decided to try once more.

Angela Clemmons

To our surprise, we conceived again—another girl. It was a little tough for me at first, admittedly. I had my heart set on a son to carry on the family name. However, I understood that this baby was a blessing from God, just like my other daughters, and excitement filled our hearts as we prepared for her arrival. On March 15, 1997, I went into labor. We were excited, eagerly awaiting the birth of our new baby girl. Having experienced childbirth twice before, I felt prepared for the pain and discomfort. Yet, I could not foresee the ordeal that lay ahead—one that would take me to the brink of death.

After hours of intense labor and what seemed like an eternity, my baby made her debut into the world! The joy of seeing her was indescribable, but my elation was short-lived. My last memory was of placing her to my breast to nurse, but then everything changed. My world went dark as I slipped into unconsciousness.

When I regained consciousness, the scene around me was absolute chaos. Doctors surrounded me, frantically requesting my husband's signature to authorize an emergency hysterectomy. I was hemorrhaging severely, and that surgery was the only way to save my life. In that critical moment, God's presence was undeniable. I prayed during my moments of consciousness, telling God that if He let me live, I would always use my voice to glorify His name. Sometimes, when things get really hard, we try to bargain with God, and this was one of those moments. I was too young to die; I just wasn't ready to go—not like that. His purpose for my life was still unfolding, but I just could not grasp the significance of this event.

In the midst of the chaos, with my life hanging by a thread, my thoughts raced. I thought of my children, my husband, and all the dreams yet to be fulfilled. The weight of unfinished business and the deep desire to see my children grow up filled me with an overwhelming will to survive. I wasn't ready to leave this world. I had so much more to give, so much more to do. The promise I made to God in those critical moments came from a place of desperation and hope. It was a plea for more time, a vow to dedicate my life to His service if He granted me another chance.

When the surgery was finally over, and I woke up in the recovery room, the fact that I had almost died began to sink in. I was grateful to be alive, to be given a second chance. The journey ahead would be challenging, but I was determined to honor the promise I made to God.

The trauma of that near-death experience, however, bound me for some time. I could not help but feel a profound sense of loss and resentment that the choice to have another child was taken from me. My mind was a whirlpool of conflicting emotions. The realization that I could no longer bear children struck at the core of my identity. In my mind, I no longer felt like a whole woman. Postpartum depression gripped me tightly, making each day a battle to even get out of bed. Day after day, I wept. I'm not sure how many days I cried. I just could not shake this cloud of sadness surrounding me.

Even though I was in deep depression, I had to function as a mother and a wife. After my six weeks of maternity leave, I had to go back to work to provide for my family. Each morning, I got up and went to work, putting on a brave face. On Sundays, I went back to church, taking solace in the familiarity of the routine. I took care of my motherly duties, all the while fighting off these dark days. I tried my best not to let my children see me cry, so I would wait until I was alone. There was a bridge that I drove over every day on my way home from work. There were moments when the darkness was so overwhelming, I contemplated driving off that bridge, just to silence the turmoil raging inside my mind.

My husband, bless his heart, tried his best to understand and support me, but the depth of my struggle was beyond his comprehension. Amid all the turmoil and despair, there was a small, persistent voice that whispered: "There is so much to live for." I had to be strong for my three daughters and my husband. Realizing I needed help, I reached out to my doctor, who prescribed antidepressant medication. Trusting that these medications would help, I took them as prescribed.

However, the medication made me feel like I was not in control. The foggy haze it created was a constant reminder that something external was managing my emotions. Deep within, I knew that medication alone wasn't the key to my complete freedom. It was God. To truly rid myself of the demons of depression that had invaded my mind and life, I needed to draw closer to Him.

I began to pray more intensely, digging into the Word of God. I recalled scriptures I had learned as a little girl, finding peace and strength in them. This was a pivotal time in my life when I began to understand that Jesus would help me if I just called on Him. Psalm

34:17 comes to mind: "The righteous cry out, and the Lord hears them; He delivers them from all their troubles." I cried out to God persistently, knowing that He was my ultimate healer and the true source of my strength.

The more I prayed and read my Bible, the more I felt God's presence comforting me. My faith began to grow stronger, and I realized that my journey to recovery was not just a physical one but a spiritual one as well. This was the turning point that allowed me to regain control over my life, not through medication alone, but through a stronger relationship with God.

I remembered my grandmother often rebuking the devil, and James 4:7 came to mind: "Submit yourselves, then, to God. Resist the devil, and he will flee from you." I started rebuking the demons of depression, commanding them to leave in the name of Jesus.

Since Jesus Christ was Lord of my life, I had the authority and power given to me by His blood. With each passing day, my strength and hope increased as I continued to read the Bible and declare my freedom. I embraced James 4:8, "Come near to God and He will come near to you," finding peace and strength in His presence. Then, one day, I woke up with a smile on the inside, a smile that bubbled up and radiated on my face. I had weathered the storm, and the demon of depression was gone! I fought depression with the weapons of faith, prayer, and the Word of God, and I emerged victorious.

These weapons are available to you as well if you have accepted Jesus Christ into your life. You have the right to call on the name of Jesus, at which demons flee! You have the sword of the Spirit and the shield of faith, as Ephesians 6 states: "Put on the full armor of God, so that you can take your stand against the devil's schemes." This journey taught me that true freedom and peace come from drawing close to God, resisting the devil, and standing firm in the power of His Word.

Chapter 6 Devotional: God's Presence During our Storms

Scripture Reading: Psalm 34:17, James 4:7-8, Ephesians 6:10-18

In the most critical moments of our lives, God's presence is undeniable. I vividly remember the day our third daughter was born, a day that should have been filled with joy but quickly turned into a battle for my life. When I hemorrhaged severely during childbirth, the doctors rushed to perform an emergency hysterectomy. It was in those frantic moments, as I lay on the brink of death, that I felt God's presence so strongly. I prayed, promising God that if He allowed me to live, I would use my voice to glorify His name. This was a desperate plea, but it was also a powerful moment of surrender and trust in God's plan for my life.

This incident brought postpartum depression; a deep darkness that seemed impossible to shake. Each day was a struggle to fulfill my roles as a wife and mother. While I was yet in despair, a persistent voice reminded me of God's purpose for my life. I turned to prayer and God's Word, finding strength in scriptures like Psalm 34:17: "The righteous cry out, and the Lord hears them; He delivers them from all their troubles."

Through persistent prayer and meditation on God's Word, I began to rebuke the spirit of depression, as James 4:7-8 instructs:

"Submit yourselves, then, to God. Resist the devil, and he will flee from you. Come near to God and He will come near to you." This spiritual battle, fought with the weapons of faith, prayer, and God's Word, led to my victory over depression.

With each prayer, my faith grew stronger, and I began to experience a peace that transcended my circumstances. One day, I woke up with an inner smile, a joy that radiated through me. The demon of depression had been defeated, not by medication alone but by the power of prayer, faith, and God's Word.

This devotional is a testament to God's faithfulness and a reminder that even in our darkest hours, we are never alone. Depression is a spirit we can fight with the powerful weapons of faith, prayer, and God's Word. God's promises are powerful and true. Just as He delivered me from the depths of depression, He will deliver you.

Persist in prayer, immerse yourself in the scriptures, and rebuke the spirit of depression in the name of Jesus. You have the authority and the right to call on His name and experience the freedom and peace that only God can provide. Trust in God's steadfast love and let His Word be your source of strength and hope.

Heartfelt Reflections

Read: Psalm 34, James 4;7-8, Ephesians 6;10-18

Reflect: In moments of crisis, surrender your fears and anxieties to God through prayer. Trust in His plan for your life, knowing that

He is with you even in the darkest times. Recognize that depression and despair are tools of the enemy. Rebuke these spirits in the name of Jesus and stand firm in your faith. Immerse yourself in the scriptures. You will find strength, comfort and power in God's word.

Journal: Reflect on a time in your life when you experienced a critical situation. Do you feel that you were fully equipped? Which of these scriptures resonate with you the most? Based on the truth of God's word, how will you apply them to your life moving forward?

Rejoice: Put on the full Armor of God as Ephesians 6:10-18 teaches. Use the sword of the Spirit, which is the Word of God, and the shield of faith to stand against the devil's schemes. Thank God that he has equipped you with the power of his word to stand strong in any situation that comes your way.

Prayer: Heavenly Father, Thank You for Your presence in my life, especially during the most challenging times. Help me to always remember that You hear my cries and deliver me from all my troubles. Strengthen my faith and help me to resist the enemy's attacks through prayer and Your Word. May I always seek you first when trouble comes my way. Help me to use spiritual weapons that you have given me, to fight, and to win. In Jesus' name. Amen.

Chapter 7

It Got Physical

CHAPTER 7

It Got Physical

In this life journey, we are constantly confronted with obstacles that threaten to hinder our progress. Think about some of the events in life you have had to overcome: financial struggles, job insecurities, and even physical attacks can test our strength and faith. Yet, despite the challenges we face, we must press on and fight the good fight of faith. Life does not stop because we encounter setbacks.

The enemy's strategy is to exploit these challenges, magnifying our struggles and sowing seeds of doubt. He aims to weaken and disconnect us from our source of strength. His attacks are not random but deliberate, targeting us where we are most vulnerable, intending to deter us from fulfilling our God-given purpose. This is why it's crucial to recognize that these battles are not just physical or circumstantial; they are deeply spiritual.

Having a shepherd chosen by God to impart wisdom and knowledge of His Word provided me with a strong foundation. It strengthened my faith and prepared me for the battles ahead. Being in an atmosphere where I learned the importance of worship and praise, and gained strong teaching about the principles and power of God, prepared me for some of the hardest experiences I would ever face.

Angela Clemmons

This firm foundation supplied me with the weapons needed to fight and the faith to believe that God would provide answers.

Active involvement in ministry has always been important to me, and my chosen path of contribution was through the ministry of song. As a member of the praise team, I found fulfillment in dancing "like David danced" unto the Lord. However, as you may know, the enemy seeks to destroy and block acts of worship because he is keenly aware of its power and impact.

When we worship, we align ourselves with God's purpose, drawing closer to His presence and invoking His power in our lives. Acts of worship are not just expressions of faith; they are spiritual battles that declare God's sovereignty and our allegiance to Him. Worship shifts atmospheres, breaks chains, and brings forth divine intervention. Our praise is a weapon. The enemy, in his relentless pursuit to steal, kill, and destroy, used a physical attack to target my worship, weaken my faith, and disrupt my connection to God.

In the winter of 2018, I began experiencing excruciating pain in my back. With a high pain tolerance, I put off seeking medical attention. A mother and wife must keep moving, you know! Despite the pain, I persisted in my role on the praise team, leading the saints into battle through worship, singing, and dancing to glorify God. I knew that my worship was a weapon, and I refused to let the pain silence my praise.

Several months passed before a consultation with an orthopedic doctor revealed a diagnosis of degenerative disc disease. This condition involves the degeneration or bulging of discs in the lower spine, leading to nerve pain. Life continued as usual pending MRI results. Surgery was an option, but first, physical therapy was tried to alleviate the pain.

Despite the diagnosis, I continued to minister. Each Sunday, I pushed through the pain, lifting my voice and moving my body in worship. It wasn't just about the physical act of singing and dancing; it was about defying the enemy's attempts to silence my praise.

In my determination to continue ministering despite the pain, I recalled a chiropractor who had provided physical therapy before. I consulted him regarding my back, hoping for relief. After discussing various options, a routine adjustment was performed, aiming to reduce the pain. However, this adjustment felt drastically different. A sharp crack reverberated through my spine, accompanied by an intense wave of pain.

Unbeknownst to the chiropractor, who had not reviewed the MRI film, my condition involved a bulging disc. The adjustment inadvertently worsened my condition, leaving me in greater agony!

Leaving the chiropractic office, I found myself in more pain than ever before. Reaching home was a monumental task. Climbing the stairs was nearly impossible as a burning sensation radiated from my buttocks, causing numbness in my leg. The pain was relentless, leading to crawling on the floor just to reach the bathroom.

This torment continued for several days. I frantically searched Google for pain centers that might offer a quick solution to this pain. I hoped a steroid shot could provide relief. Mobility had become so limited that crawling and sliding were now my only options for getting around.

With the help of a supportive husband, a visit to the pain center was arranged. The trip was agonizing. Unable to walk down the stairs, I slid on my belly and was carried to the car. Since sitting was impossible, the ride to the pain center was spent lying on my belly with my legs awkwardly bent behind me. Every bump in the road sent jolts of pain through my body, and every stoplight felt like an eternity. I clung to the hope that relief was around the corner.

Arriving at the pain center, we checked in, only to be informed that it would take 3-5 days to obtain authorization for treatment. I was crushed. Sent home without help or pain pills, feeling hopeless, I faced the prospect of enduring unbearable pain for several more days. Tears freely flowed as desperation set in. That night, I told my husband that if we didn't find immediate help by the next day, I would have to check myself into the hospital.

This was a moment where all the praying, fasting, and seeking had to be put into action. As the sun rose the next morning, I fervently prayed to God, pleading for His guidance and assistance. Miraculously, an orthopedic doctor was found who agreed to see me immediately. Summoning the strength for one more low crawl from the bedroom to the stairs, and then lying on my belly in the back seat of the car, I began to see a glimmer of hope. Though I was still unsure of what was wrong, I felt deep down that help was on the way.

Arriving at the orthopedic doctor's office, I struggled inside and collapsed onto the floor. The doctor and staff quickly evaluated the situation. It was discovered that the previous adjustment had shattered the disc, with fragments lodged into the sciatic nerve. Finally, there was clarity on the cause of the pain! The doctors were astounded by my ability to function under such conditions. Without hesitation, they rushed me to the nearest hospital by ambulance, where I was admitted, with emergency back surgery scheduled for the next day!

In the moments before the surgery, a flood of thoughts raced through my mind as I signed the papers, terrified at the possibility of paralysis. This was not an elective surgery but a necessary reaction to the urgency of my condition. The weight of impending surgery was heavy, but even though I felt fear, I clung to the hope found in scriptures. Comforting verses like Psalm 23:4, "Even though I walk through the valley of the shadow of death, I will fear no evil, for You are with me; Your rod and Your staff, they comfort me," and 2 Timothy 1:7, "For God has not given us a spirit of fear, but of power and of love and of a sound mind," provided peace and reassurance as I faced the unknown.

The surgery was a success, but a challenging recovery lay ahead. Weeks of physical therapy awaited, but through it all, God was faithful. Despite lingering numbness in my right leg and foot, the gratitude for being able to walk, run, and praise God overshadowed any discomfort. After months of rehabilitation, I rejoined the praise team, lifting my voice in thanksgiving!

This experience reinforced my belief that God can answer prayers quickly and powerfully. Often, life's challenges bring us to a breaking point where we cannot endure any more. It is in these times that our faith must be tested. In my most desperate moment, when no one else could help, God intervened. Praying fervently and using my faith led me to a doctor with an immediate opening and a surgery slot the next day! This divine intervention was clear evidence of God working on my behalf. The back surgeon became my angel, performing a miracle through his skilled hands. Witnessing this firsthand solidified my belief in God's healing power. No one could convince me otherwise—I had seen it with my own eyes.

Not long after, another attack. Another surgery became imminent. I noticed during my singing that there was a strange trill in my high soprano register. It wasn't painful, but it gave a raspy rattle to my otherwise silky-smooth soprano voice. A friend recommended that I consult with an Ear, Nose, and Throat specialist. Reluctantly, I made the appointment, nervous about what they might find. The procedure was extremely uncomfortable. They inserted a scope through my nose, down my throat, and into my vocal box to view my vocal cords. A nodule was found on my vocal cord. Despite my faith that God had not given me a spirit of fear, I was terrified. My voice was my instrument of praise, and all sorts of worries filled my mind. What would the surgery be like? Would I lose my voice? Singing in praise and worship was my life, and it defined my identity.

The impending vocal cord surgery weighed heavily on my mind. Would my voice emerge from this operation the same as before, or would it be forever altered? Could I still sing and pour out my heart in praise as I used to? Would I matter as much to others and to myself? Questions swirled in my head, filled with uncertainty and fear. But even in my doubts, there was determination. I resolved to get through

I Thought I Lost

this and return to the worship songs that filled my soul. The day of the vocal cord surgery arrived, accompanied by nervousness. The doctor's decision to perform the procedure while I was awake only added to my anxiety.

The first sensation was the numbing of my voice box—a unique, creeping cold sensation that seemed to close off my throat. As the numbing medicine was injected through the scope, I found myself gurgling, almost gagging, desperate for air. It was a moment of suffocating panic, worsened by the horrible smell of burning flesh as the high-intensity laser burned away the nodule on my vocal cord.

In that intense discomfort, I turned my thoughts to the familiar words of the 23rd Psalm. "The LORD is my shepherd; I shall not want. He makes me lie down in green pastures..." I repeated these verses in my mind like a lifeline, clinging to the promise of God's presence with me, even as I felt utterly alone in that surgery room.

With no hand to squeeze for comfort, I delved deeper into the well of scripture hidden in my heart. God's word brought me peace. The scriptures I had read and studied now took on new significance, their words of healing and comfort becoming more real than ever before. It was a test of not just my physical endurance but also my spiritual resilience.

After the surgery came a period of vocal rest—a silent interlude. No speaking, whispering, or humming—any sound could risk reinjury. It was a frustrating and isolating time, filled with doubts and fears. What if I couldn't sing again? Had I truly given my all to God, as I had promised on my deathbed years ago?

Angela Clemmons

Through 12 weeks of voice therapy, these questions weighed heavily on my mind. The memory of my earlier promise to God haunted me. Had I truly lived up to it? And why did it seem that life kept throwing these challenges at me—first the back surgery, now this?

Yet, even in my doubts, there was a growing realization. These trials, as difficult as they were, had the potential to become testimonies. They were building something within me—a deeper understanding of faith and strength. I clung to the belief that God is a healer, that if He had done it before, He could do it again.

Through the long days of therapy and the silent nights of contemplation, I found myself drawing closer to God. The tests were not punishments but opportunities for me to grow in my relationship with Christ. And as I emerged from the darkness of uncertainty, I knew that whatever the outcome, my faith had been tested and found strong. These challenges would indeed become testimonies, reminders of the unshakable faith that carried me through.

Chapter 7 Devotional: Trusting God for Healing

Scripture Reading:

Isaiah 53:5: "But he was pierced for our transgressions, he was crushed for our iniquities; the punishment that brought us peace was on him, and by his wounds we are healed."

Psalm 147:3: "He heals the brokenhearted and binds up their wounds."

1 Peter 5:10: "And the God of all grace, who called you to his eternal glory in Christ, after you have suffered a little while, will himself restore you and make you strong, firm, and steadfast."

Life's battles often come unexpectedly, testing our faith and resilience. Yet, these moments are precisely when we must lean into God's promises, trusting Him for guidance and healing. Our struggles are not just physical or circumstantial but are deeply spiritual, requiring us to fully rely on God's wisdom and strength.

In the midst of severe back pain, which was later diagnosed as degenerative disc disease, I experienced a moment where all the praying, fasting, and seeking had to be put into action. The pain was unbearable, yet I held on to God's promises, knowing that He was my healer. As I fervently prayed for His guidance and assistance.

My situation required immediate back surgery, and as I faced the possibility of paralysis, scriptures like Psalm 23:4 and 2 Timothy 1:7 provided peace and reassurance. The surgery was successful, and though the recovery was challenging, God was faithful throughout. Despite lingering numbness, I rejoiced in my ability to walk and praise God again.

This experience reinforced my belief in God's healing power and His ability to answer prayers quickly and powerfully. When another health issue arose—a nodule on my vocal cord—I again turned to God. Despite my fear of losing my voice, I trusted Him. The surgery was daunting, but God was with me, and my voice was restored. Through these trials, I witnessed firsthand the power of prayer and God's faithfulness.

Whatever battles you face today, trust in God's promises. He is with you in every struggle, offering guidance and comfort. Lean into His strength and find peace knowing that things are working for your good, according to Romans 8:28. May your faith in His word sustain you and lead you to your victory. Amen.

Heartfelt Reflections

Read: Isaiah 53:5, Psalm 147:3, and 1 Peter 5:10. These scriptures highlight God's healing power and His promise to restore us.

Reflect: Consider a time when you faced a significant challenge. How did you see God's hand at work? How did your faith sustain you through the difficulty?

Journal: Reflect on the challenges you are currently facing or have faced in the past. How will you use the scriptures from Isaiah 53:5, Psalm 147:3, and 1 Peter 5:10 to overcome these battles in your life? Which of these scriptures resonate with you the most and give you the strength and power to persevere? Write down your thoughts and any personal revelations you receive from meditating on these verses.

Rejoice:

Spend time in worship, thanking God for His promises of healing. Praise Him for the victories He has brought you through and for the strength He provides in every battle.

Prayer:

Heavenly Father, Thank You for being our healer and sustainer. When we face physical and emotional battles, help us to trust in Your promises and lean on Your strength. Remind us that our worship is a powerful weapon against the enemy. We praise You for the victories You have given us and for the assurance that You are always with us. In Jesus' name, Amen.

I Thought I Lost

Heartfelt Reflections

Chapter 8

Lost Identity - Finding Myself

I Thought I Lost

CHAPTER 8
Lost Identity Finding Myself

As mothers, raising children and managing families, we often lose touch with our identities. Our sense of self becomes intertwined with our roles as caregivers, spouses, church members, and employees— everything except our own essence. It took many years to grow into the person I am today, and this transformation was far from immediate. My journey of rediscovery truly began when my kids left home, and I found a small direct sales business that reignited my sense of purpose.

For as long as I can remember, my identity has been wrapped up in my roles as a mom, wife, and employee. Becoming a mother at 20 years old marked the beginning of a significant identity shift. This loss of identity wasn't sudden but gradual. I was a dedicated mother, always attentive to my children's needs. They were well-clothed, and I cooked wholesome meals for them and my husband—all while juggling one or more jobs. I've always been a go-getter and high achiever.

How I loved being a mother! My three daughters were my pride and joy. I took them to church and raised them in the Lord, as the Bible instructs. My husband and I worked together seamlessly, adjusting our schedules to ensure our girls were well cared for. We made sure they could participate in activities that nurtured their talents and interests—dance classes, recitals, swim lessons, and ball games filled our calendar. We wanted them to have fun and enjoy their childhood, ensuring they grew up well-rounded.

Balancing work, managing a household, and raising three children isn't easy. Mothers often put their dreams on hold. Who can think about dreams when you're constantly caring for little ones? Or so I thought. The joy and fulfillment of watching my daughters grow and thrive were immeasurable, but I gradually realized that my own dreams and identity had taken a back seat.

Our family was rooted in faith. Church attendance was regular—every Sunday, Tuesday, and Friday. Ministry was a significant part of our lives, and daily prayer with the children was a cherished practice, aiming to raise them in God's ways. Church wasn't just a building but the foundation of our lives, where we learned and embraced God's principles for living.

Active involvement in ministry was a shared commitment. Serving on the praise team most Sundays, using my gifted and anointed voice, brought joy and fulfillment. Rehearsals were frequent, with the children always by my side. Each service and rehearsal was a testament to dedication and faithfulness.

The church served as a classroom for learning how to be a good wife, raise children wisely, and embody the virtues of the Proverbs 31 woman. Lessons on respecting my husband and other values gleaned from the church community played a vital role in maintaining a strong marriage. We were taught the importance of a wife's respect for her husband, a cornerstone of a thriving marriage. As a devoted wife, I made sure my husband had everything he needed. Through these experiences, the power of prayer and the Holy Spirit became integral in our daily lives.

Family and faith formed the foundation of my identity, but my professional life also demanded a significant part of me. It was another facet of myself dedicated to serving others. I was fortunate to have rewarding jobs where exceeding expectations was the norm. Hard work and dedication defined my daily routine. I took Colossians 3:23 seriously: "Whatever you do, work at it with all your heart, as working for the Lord, not for human masters." This verse guided my work ethic, and I poured my heart into everything I did. My identity became intertwined with my job—a high achiever focused on the mission, often at the expense of personal self-care.

In this relentless pursuit of excellence, prioritizing others over myself became second nature. Attending to everyone else's needs, mothers often neglect their own well-being. Self-care was nearly nonexistent, with moments of relaxation few and far between. Choir rehearsals, rather than personal pampering, became my form of self-care.

This is the life of a mother: attending to everyone else, rarely taking care of ourselves. We are mostly givers, not takers, nurturing by nature. We embrace this role, and we excel at it. Our identity as caregivers fuels us as long as we're deeply immersed in those roles.

The loss of identity we experience as mothers is gradual. We pour ourselves into our families, work, and ministries, often forgetting to invest in ourselves. The roles of mother, wife, and employee fill our days and shape our sense of self. But there comes a time when the children grow up and leave home. Suddenly, the roles that once defined us no longer do. It's in this space that we begin to rediscover who we are.

When my children left home, I faced an unfamiliar quiet. The bustling household I once managed was now still. It was both a relief and a challenge. I began to ask myself, "Now, what do I do with myself?" I was still working, but there was extra time on my hands. The silence was unfamiliar, unusual now that my children were gone.

This newfound silence allowed me to reflect on who I was beyond the roles I had played for so many years. It was then that I stumbled upon a small direct sales company that happened to promote dry nail polish. Initially, it was something to occupy my extra time, but it soon became much more—it became a pathway to rediscovering myself, a pathway to purpose.

Starting this business was like a breath of fresh air. Embracing something new that I had never done before, I began to meet many women just like myself. This venture helped me realize that I could be dynamic. My business helped me step out of my comfort zone like never before.

Through this business, I learned the importance of self-care and helped many other women incorporate it into their lives. Working in this business, I became more confident and outgoing, connecting with people through a smile that radiated the joy of the Lord. I excelled, building a solid team and earning three all-expense-paid trips to Jamaica, Mexico, and the Dominican Republic.

My success came from applying principles found in the Word of God. Psalm 1:3 says, "That person is like a tree planted by streams of water, which yields its fruit in season and whose leaf does not wither—whatever they do prospers." Praying over my business and grounding it in scripture brought prosperity. The skills I had learned in my years of employment translated into success in my social selling business as well.

This journey of rediscovery was gradual, but this business helped me understand that my identity wasn't solely tied to being a mother, a wife, or an employee. I learned to find joy in activities that were solely for me. One of the most significant aspects of this business journey was helping other women see what took me over 40 years to see: the importance of prioritizing self-care. Realizing that taking care of myself wasn't selfish but necessary was a major lesson learned.

As a woman of faith, I know that God has a purpose for me beyond my roles as a mother and wife. It took many years, but I've grown into the woman God created me to be. Now, I can encourage and inspire other women, helping them realize their identities in Christ. This journey has been long, but it's been worth every step. Today, I'm not just a mother, a wife, or an employee—I am Angela Clemmons, a daughter of God.

Reflecting on this journey, every step, struggle, and victory has shaped who I am today. The transition from a bustling household to a quieter, reflective space was a pivotal moment. It was in this silence that I discovered layers of my identity buried under years of nurturing and caregiving. Embracing this new venture brought a surge of passion and purpose.

Engaging in this business, I connected with countless women, each with their own story of identity and rediscovery. We shared experiences, learned from one another, and found strength in our collective journey. This community of women became a source of inspiration and support, forging lifelong connections.

The trips and accolades weren't just rewards; they were evidence that with Christ, all things are possible. These achievements marked my growth and transformation. They broadened my horizons, allowing me to see the world and my place in it from a new perspective. Mentoring others brought a sense of fulfillment as I witnessed empowerment and confidence spreading among the women I worked with.

Reflecting on finding and knowing myself better, I'm grateful for uncovering God's purpose waiting for me to discover. The journey of self-discovery has laid a solid foundation, paving the way for deeper exploration of God's purpose for my life. It's a journey of faith, growth, and continual transformation.

Journal: Discovering Your Identity in God's Word

Scripture: Psalm 139:13-14, Ephesians 2:10, Proverbs 31

As a mother and woman deeply engaged in parenting, nurturing, and various roles, I often found myself wondering about my own identity. God's Word speaks volumes about who we are in His eyes—fearfully and wonderfully made, created with a unique purpose. Psalm 139:13-14 reminds me that I am intricately woven by God Himself, and Ephesians 2:10 assures me that I am His handiwork, designed to fulfill His divine plan.

Reflecting on my journey, I recall situations where roles as a mother, spouse, and employee many times overshadowed my individual identity. I experienced seasons where the demands of caregiving and daily responsibilities left little room for personal exploration. Yet, God's Word helped me to see beyond these roles and embrace the identity He had ordained for me.

Proverbs 31 paints a portrait of a woman who embodies strength, dignity, and wisdom—a woman whose worth far exceeds rubies. This chapter is a reflection of God's vision for His daughters. It challenges us to embrace the qualities of the Proverbs 31 woman, not as an unattainable standard, but as a system of empowerment rooted in God's grace.

In reflecting on these scriptures, I have come to understand that God's purpose for me goes beyond the roles that society expects me to fulfill as a wife, mother, and employee. I found renewed purpose in my direct sales business, experiencing God opening doors , revealing new facets of my identity that reflect His glory. Whether through my career, personal passions, or ministry opportunities, each step showed me more about His intricate plan and design for my life.

Today, I invite you to journey with me in embracing the truth of God's Word. Let's look at ourselves through His eyes—valued, cherished, and equipped for every good work (2 Timothy 3:17). As we walk together, may we grow in our identity in Christ, embodying all that His word says we are to be and accomplishing the good work he planned for us. Let's view the virtues of the Proverbs 31 woman not as a checklist, but as a reflection of our ongoing transformation into the woman God created us to be.

Heartfelt Reflections:

Read: Psalm 139, Ephesians 2:10, Proverbs31

Reflect: Consider moments in your life when your identity felt overshadowed by your roles as a mother, wife, or employee. How did you navigate these seasons? Reflect on any opportunities or challenges that sparked moments where you felt there was a need to discover yourself.

Journal: Reflecting on Proverbs 31, which virtues of the Proverbs 31 woman resonate most with you? How can you begin to incorporate these virtues into your daily life and interactions with others? Consider 2 Timothy 3:17 which assures us that we are equipped for every good work through God's Word. How can you apply this assurance to overcome challenges or pursue new opportunities in your life?

Rejoice: Rejoice in the journey of discovering and embracing the unique identity God has ordained for you. His plans are perfect. Thank Him in advance for guiding you towards a life filled with purpose.

Prayer:

Heavenly Father, Thank You for creating me fearfully and wonderfully. Help me to see myself through Your eyes and to embrace the identity You have designed for me. Guide me in discovering the purpose You have placed in my heart, beyond the roles I fulfill. May

Angela Clemmons

I apply the truth of your word to fulfill all the great plans that you have for me. In Jesus' name, Amen.

Heartfelt Reflections

Chapter 9

Purpose Discovered

CHAPTER 9

Purpose Discovered

You are never too old to uncover your purpose and design for your life. As a mother, I recognized that part of my purpose was to raise my children in the Lord because this is right according to scripture. It was also my purpose to be an example to them of how a mother and wife should operate, to teach them and rear them to the best of my ability while they were in my household. I know in my heart that I raised my children the best way I knew how, and I am very proud of the strong, wise young women they have become. I'm so proud of them.

Helping others has always been a passion. Sharing knowledge to help others become better became evident through opportunities to mentor and train women in direct sales and even at work. Being a giver and sharer is by design, a reflection of God's handiwork. I found joy in seeing others grow, in witnessing their transformation and success. It was then that I realized my calling was based on serving and uplifting others, and this has brought a sense of fulfillment to my life.

When I look back over all the challenges I have encountered in life, I ask myself, why has the enemy tried so hard to destroy my life? Why did I experience electrical shock at five years old? What was the purpose of almost losing my life during childbirth? Why did the enemy

I Thought I Lost

try so hard to stop my worship by inflicting physical attacks? Perhaps it was that promise to God when I was on my deathbed, that if He allowed me to live, I would always use my voice to give Him glory.

Active involvement in church has always been a cornerstone of my life. Singing for the Lord, whether in the choir or on the praise team, was my lifelong ministry gift. The talent and gifting were evident, and I thought my purpose in life was to sing on the praise team and the choir. Excellence in this service to God was fulfilling, yet during a season when I was not singing, I felt like I was missing something.

Recently, I discovered an identity outside of my children, but I had not yet uncovered the depth of my identity in Christ. Although I had been a praying and fasting woman for many years and considered myself a mature Christian, I had not inquired of God who I truly was as His daughter. This held the key to understanding my divine calling from God.

You have probably heard the term that the Lord works in mysterious ways. Let me share with you how I found out that He truly does. In February of 2023, I received a call stating that my grandmother had been diagnosed with stage 4 lung cancer. This diagnosis stunned our family. We had no idea of the severity of the situation, and it was important for us to see her right away. We hustled to make plans to be with her, wanting to see how she was doing, spend time with her, and glean from her wisdom. I connected with family from all over the country—many cousins, aunts, and uncles I had not seen in over twenty years. Within a week's time, we had almost planned a whole family reunion around visiting my grandmother.

It took two flights to get to Birmingham, Alabama, and then an hour and a half drive to reach her, but we were determined. When we arrived, grandmother was in great spirits and doing very well. Honestly, she did not even look like she was sick with cancer. We spent a few days with her, fellowshipping and catching up with each other. The last time many of us had seen one another was in childhood. It was a special time for us all.

Grandmother was a woman of God—a praying woman, a saint! She did the work of the Lord, and was well known in her community and church. She was a writer and had a monthly column in the Gadsden Times. She also loved music and taught piano to students young and old. Grandmother was always serving people both inside and outside of the church walls. So, even though she was not feeling her best, at 93 years old and battling cancer, we knew we were going to church with her on Sunday! I had my clothes ready, and Sunday service was amazing. A host of our family was in attendance to praise the Lord for the time we had with her that weekend. I know you are wondering what this has to do with recognizing my divine purpose. Keep reading—I'm getting to it.

Most people, when traveling a long way to visit family, try to see everyone they can while there, just in case it's a long time before returning. With several aunts, uncles, and cousins in Gadsden, I intended to see as many people as possible. After visiting with my grandmother, my cousins and I spent about an hour catching up with

I Thought I Lost

my Uncle Rex. It was nothing out of the norm—just family enjoying good fellowship. There was another uncle and aunt I needed to see before making the trek back to Raleigh, but this visit turned out to be more than I had bargained for.

God had something so unexpected lined up for us. Isaiah 55:8-9 says, "My thoughts are not your thoughts, my ways are not your ways." I could not fathom what was going to take place as we walked into my Uncle Robert's home. I arrived with my brother and cousins, Lela, Tarsha, and Myeshia. We entered as usual, with smiles and elation, sharing hugs with Uncle Robert and Aunt Wanetta. I sat down on the corner of the couch near my aunt as we began to talk about old times. She asked many questions, and we shared with her. Minutes passed, and we were enjoying our time together, but soon the atmosphere began to shift.

The Spirit of God entered that room, and my aunt began to prophesy. I had not seen my aunt since I was a little girl, and I had no idea she was a prophet. She started from the left side of the room, one by one, calling out things that God was showing her. We had walked into a spiritual ambush. This visit turned into a prayer and deliverance session!

I sat on the couch watching in awe of what was happening. The house was filled with prayer and weeping as my aunt continued prophesying. I remained in my same spot in the corner of the couch, praying in the Holy Spirit. I thought to myself, "I'm good, so I'll just keep praying for everyone else." Before I knew it, the attention had shifted to me. Aunt Wanetta looked my way and began to call me out.

She told me that I was compromising. At that time, I was hungering for a deeper experience with God. She spoke about things hidden deep within my heart, addressing insecurities I held inside, places where I felt hidden and needed to be free. She told me that my life was fake and declared that I had an assignment: to speak what the Lord wants spoken.

This was an experience unlike any I had ever had before. It confounds me to think that God brought me all these miles to give me this message. But I believed it and received it right then. 2 Chronicles 20:20 declares, "Believe in the Lord your God, so shall ye be established; believe in His prophets, and so shall ye prosper." God revealed my purpose right there in those moments at 51 years old. I was transformed by her prophecy and had received my marching orders.

Upon returning home, a new sense of purpose filled me. I began to fervently study God's word, not just for personal growth, but as a conduit—someone called to lead others into victory. It was crucial for me to walk boldly as a servant of God because I was now on assignment. My focus became strictly on feasting on the Word of God, revisiting areas in my life where I still felt hidden. I realized I had to come out of hiding so that I could help other women do the same.

Proverbs 31 took on a new meaning for me. I had read it many times over the years, but as I delved deeper into its verses, I realized how strong I was—how strong I had always been. The Proverbs 31 woman was a boss. She worked hard, owned businesses, and cared for her family. She wasn't just humble and holy; she was powerful! I realized that's who I've always been, and it was time to walk in it! Isaiah 60:1 says to "Arise and Shine." This scripture, which I had read before, now spoke to me in a new way. I realized I was not supposed to be hidden behind my past—my mistakes as a youth, in parenting, or even in marriage. This verse reminded me that God's light is shining on me. The Hebrew dictionary describes light as brightness, enlightenment, happiness, and cheerfulness. All of this described me.

This truth was in God's Word, and it belonged to me. I just had to dig in and find it. Many people go through their whole lives not experiencing the fullness of what God has planned and prepared for those who love Him because they don't know all the specifics. But I was determined to uncover every truth, every promise that God had for me. I wanted to ensure that I was walking fully in the path He had laid out, not just for myself, but to guide others into their own victories. Revelations 12 says that we have overcome by the blood of the Lamb and the words of our testimony. We all have a story. My story is meant to help others overcome problems in their lives. God helped me learn through His Word how to come out of hiding and walk in the purpose He had planned for me so long ago.

Now, I declare to you: it is time for you to come out of hiding. I want to share with you how, just like me, you can come out now. First and foremost, you must know your true identity in Christ. 1 Peter 2:9 in The Passion Translation declares that we are God's chosen treasure—set apart as God's devoted ones. He has called us out of darkness into His marvelous light. God brought us out for His glory. As women of virtue, our lives are more valuable than precious jewels according to Proverbs 31. We are considered royalty, not because of possessions, but because we were born into a royal family when we accepted Jesus Christ.

Fearfully and wonderfully made is how we are described—God's greatest creation. These are truths you must know about yourself so that when people come to you with lies and accusations, you can declare what the Word says about you. You can stand tall and walk in authority, knowing you are the apple of God's eye, strong, and an overcomer.

As I prepared to walk in my newly discovered purpose, I realized it required letting go of some things from my past. Letting go of the past may seem impossible, but the Word of God is life! Isaiah 43:18 admonishes us to forget the past; do not remember the old because God is about to do something new. The way He brought you out before will not compare to what He is about to do in your life. In order to move forward, you must stop looking backward. God says He will make a pathway through your wilderness and rivers in the desert. Take the Word of God to heart and do what it says. Stop giving power to the past and trust in the power of God. He wants you to prosper above all things. His thoughts toward us are not evil but of peace, to give us a bright future. Stand on that Word.

Lastly, we must spend time in prayer and in God's presence if we want to know His plans for us. Jeremiah 33:3 tells us, "Call to me and I will answer you and tell you great and unsearchable things you do not know." This scripture assures us that God longs to reveal His profound plans to us, far beyond what our minds can conceive.

Spending time in His presence opens doors to divine revelations and insights that are essential for our journey.

If you need peace, Psalm 29:11 promises, "The Lord gives strength to his people; the Lord blesses his people with peace." In God's presence, there is not just peace, but an abundance of it—peace that surpasses all understanding and guards our hearts and minds (Philippians 4:7).

As I close this chapter, I want to encourage you that whatever you need for any situation is found in the Word of God. Every promise inside the Word belongs to you. Find it, study it, meditate on it, and apply it to your life—and watch things change.

In these pages, I've glimpsed the power of God's process for living a victorious life, rooted in biblical principles. It guides us to success through meditation on God's Word, faithful application of His teachings, and the pursuit of His divine purpose in our lives. This approach has shaped my journey and empowered me to walk boldly in my purpose as a daughter of God. As we move forward, I look forward to exploring more deeply how this pathway to true success can ignite your path as well.

Chapter 9 Devotional: Embracing God's Divine Purpose

Scripture Reading: Jeremiah 29:11

"For I know the plans I have for you," declares the Lord, "plans to prosper you and not to harm you, plans to give you hope and a future."

— Jeremiah 29:11 (NIV)

Devotional:

Have you ever wondered about your divine purpose? Perhaps you've faced challenges that made you question why certain things happen. Reflecting on my life, I often asked, "Why has the enemy tried so hard to destroy my life?" From childhood accidents to near-death experiences, it felt like the adversary was determined to derail my destiny. But through every trial, I learned that God's hand was upon me, guiding me towards His divine purpose.

In a transformative experience, I found myself visiting family, not knowing that God had orchestrated this trip to reveal a profound truth about my calling. During a visit with my aunt, a prophet, I received a powerful prophecy. She spoke to the depths of my heart, addressing hidden insecurities and declaring that I was compromising my true potential.

This revelation was a turning point. I realized that I had been living a life that wasn't fully aligned with God's plan for me. It was a call to come out of hiding, to embrace the identity God had given me, and to walk boldly in His light. Isaiah 60:1 says, "Arise and shine, for your light has come, and the glory of the Lord rises upon you." This verse became my anthem. I understood that I was meant to shine, not just for myself, but to lead others into their own victories.

As women, we often wear many hats—mother, wife, business owner, friend. In the midst of these roles, it's easy to lose sight of our individual identity and purpose. But God has uniquely designed each of us with a specific calling. Ephesians 2:10 reminds us, "For we are God's handiwork, created in Christ Jesus to do good works, which God prepared in advance for us to do." We are chosen, treasured, and set apart. 1 Peter 2:9 declares that we are a royal priesthood, called out of darkness into God's marvelous light. Understanding our worth and identity in Christ empowers us to walk in our calling with confidence.

As we close this devotional, I encourage you to seek God earnestly to discover His purpose for your life. Let go of any limiting beliefs or past mistakes that may be holding you back. Have confidence in the truth that you are fearfully and wonderfully made, with a unique calling that only you can fulfill. Trust that God's plans for you are good, filled with hope and a future. Step boldly into your destiny, knowing that He is with you every step of the way.

Heartfelt Reflections:

Read: Jeremiah 29:11, Isaiah 60:1, 1 Peter 2:9, Isaiah 43:18-19

Reflect: As we embrace our divine purpose, let us remember that every promise in God's Word is ours. By studying, meditating, and applying His Word, we align ourselves with His perfect will and experience the fullness of His blessings. Jeremiah 33:3 promises that when we call to God, He will answer and reveal great and unsearchable things. Regular prayer and meditation on His Word are essential to understanding His divine plans for us. Together, let's rise and shine, reflecting God's glory, living a life of destined purpose!

Journal: Reflecting on the scriptures in the devotional, how has God revealed His purpose in your life through past experiences. Describe a moment in your life when you felt God's hand guiding you to your purpose. Based on the truth of these scriptures, what new steps can you take today to move closer to fulfilling God's purpose for your life?

Rejoice: Rejoice in the truth that you are a God's chosen treasure. You have unlimited power within you to achieve anything you put your mind to. As long as there is breath in your body, you are still on your path to Purpose!

Prayer:

Heavenly Father, Thank You for the unique purpose You've designed for each of us. Help us to embrace our identity in Christ, let go of our past, and seek Your presence daily. Reveal Your plans for us and give us the courage to walk boldly in Your light. May our lives reflect Your glory and lead others to discover their own divine purpose. In Jesus' name, Amen.

Heartfelt Reflections

Chapter 10

We Win- In the End

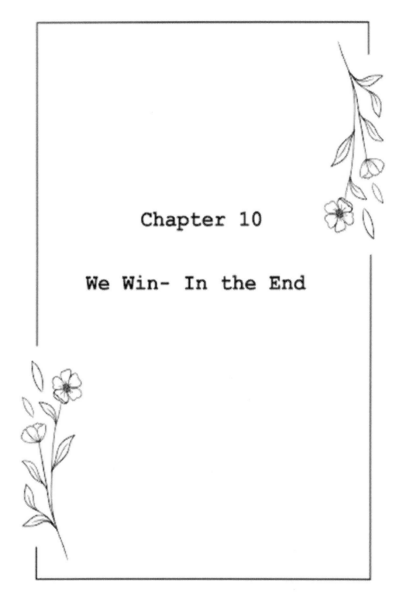

CHAPTER 10
We Win – In the End

Reflecting on my 52 years of life, I see a journey marked by countless attempts to cancel my divine purpose. This book has chronicled the many battles: the battle with shame and condemnation, the countless times I wanted to hide from the world, and the moments when I felt like giving up, believing I had nothing left to offer. The common thread in these attacks was an effort to halt the work God had ordained for me. Yet, the fundamental truth endures: when God has a purpose and a plan for your life, no weapon formed against you will prosper. God equips us with the necessary tools to fight back, and it is our responsibility to use them.

Each chapter of this book has delved into the struggles and triumphs I've experienced. From the days of feeling unworthy and shackled by shame to moments of profound revelation and divine intervention; my journey is a testament to God's unwavering faithfulness. Writing this book has illuminated how, as a child, I had no control over outcomes. But God had already chosen me, and I was blessed to have intercessors—my grandmothers—praying for me. Their prayers laid a foundation of faith in action, setting the tone for my life. This highlights the importance of intercession. As parents and grandparents, we must pray fervently for our families. Sharing Christ with our children and being examples before them plants seeds that will sprout and flourish.

The power of prayer and intercession cannot be overstated. I vividly remember the nights my grandmothers would spend in prayer, their voices softly rising in fervent supplication. They believed in the power of prayer to change circumstances, and their faith was not in vain. Their prayers carried me through many dark valleys, and their legacy of faith became a firm foundation for my spiritual life. As I grew and started to move independently, I had to cultivate my personal relationship with Christ. The exposure to God from my mother and grandmothers was my foundation, but I needed to grow and experience God for myself. Strengthening my relationship with Christ through reading His word and prayer sustained me, especially during my time in Saudi Arabia during Desert Storm. Trusting in God's word was my defense, helping me remain strong and unafraid.

During Desert Storm, I was stationed in Saudi Arabia, surrounded by uncertainty and fear. It was a physical and spiritual desert, a place where my faith was tested daily. In those moments of isolation and danger, I clung to God's promises. The scripture became my lifeline, a source of strength and hope. In life, we face desert experiences—times when our wells seem dry, and there is no water in sight. We feel empty and without answers. Just as God's word sustained me in the physical desert, it sustains us in life's deserts of overwhelm and confusion. Isaiah 43:19 declares that God will make a way in the wilderness and rivers in the desert. God moves when we put our faith into action by knowing His word and implementing it in our lives.

The deserts of life can be daunting, but they are also places of profound growth. It is in these dry, barren places that we learn to rely completely on God. We discover that even in the most challenging circumstances, God's provision is abundant. Praising God while we are within our circumstances is crucial. I found that I praised the most during my physical attacks, perhaps because the enemy tried so hard to stop my praise. 2 Chronicles 20:21-25 illustrates the power of praise. When Judah faced conflict, Jehoshaphat appointed men to sing praises to the LORD, saying, "Give thanks to the LORD, for his love endures forever." The LORD set ambushes against their enemies because the people of Judah praised Him. This teaches us a powerful lesson: when trials and tribulations come, we must reach deep inside and use our weapons of stored worship, praise, and God's promises to fight back. When the enemy is defeated, we are not only victorious but have the power to reclaim all that was stolen from us.

Praise is a weapon, a powerful tool that shifts our focus from our problems to God's greatness. It reminds us of His sovereignty and love. Throughout my life, especially during my most difficult times, praise has been my anchor. As you see, we all have a story. The purpose of this book—my story—is to help you overcome by the words of my testimony. All of these experiences, my becoming pregnant as a teenager, experiencing depressions, thoughts of suicide, identity crisis, and shame could not stop the purpose of God in my life. As Christians, our salvation gives us access to help, and power beyond our understanding which gives us the tenacity to overcome and ensures our success. We do not have to go through life being plagued by our past and haunted by our mistakes.

Angela Clemmons

My story is one of redemption and resilience. Each chapter reflects a part of my journey, filled with moments of doubt and despair, but also of incredible victories and divine encounters. Many people believe that the main benefit of salvation is simply to go to heaven. They receive salvation but still hold on to feelings of doubt and failure. They get saved for the sake of heaven but live their lives with the same feelings of unworthiness, defeat, and condemnation. Romans 8:1-2 encourages us that when we become new in Christ, there is no condemnation and that we are made free from the law of sin and death. Christ died not just for our life in heaven, but for us to live an abundant life here on earth.

Salvation is more than a ticket to heaven; it is a transformation that begins the moment we accept Christ. It is a journey of becoming, of shedding old identities and embracing our new selves in Him. As Christians, we can live a victorious life, free of doubt and fear, free of shame, and full of faith. A life of success, if you will. During my various life events detailed in this book, it would appear that I was losing. Having to leave college to raise my daughters, it may appear that I was losing. Emergency back surgery, it appeared I was losing. Not being aware of my purpose. It would appear that through all of the trials, I was losing. But God was refining me. He was building me up, strengthening me, training me through learning His word, meditating on it, and applying it to my life. Even though it looked like I was losing, I was winning the battle every time. I will forever give thanks to the Lord for giving me a revelation of what it takes to win and have success in my life.

I Thought I Lost

Life's battles often disguise our victories. What looks like defeat can be God's way of refining us, preparing us for greater things. Each trial is an opportunity for growth and transformation. You may have experienced difficult situations in your life. Maybe you are still wrestling with past mistakes or feelings of unworthiness. I want to declare to you that you are not losing. Just like I overcame every obstacle that was thrown in my path, you can do the same. It is your right to live a life of success as a believer. There is a recipe for living a victorious life.

I'll end my story by sharing three powerful tools to help you live a life of joy and success:

1. **Know Your Identity in Christ**: was life-changing when I fully understood that I was God's masterpiece, as Ephesians 2:10 declares, called to do the good things He planned for us long ago. This revelation transformed my perception of myself and my purpose. 1 Peter 2:9 details that we are chosen and that God has called us out of darkness to experience His marvelous light! You are God's best creation—an original. There is no one like you! It does not matter what the world says about you. What matters is what the Word says about you! Embracing this truth allowed me to walk confidently in the path God set for me, unbothered by external opinions or internal doubts.

2. **Fix Your Thoughts**: How you think determines your outcome in life in so many ways. Proverbs 23:7 says that as a man thinks in his heart, so is he. The heart in the Bible is

described as our mind. Our thoughts are powerful, shaping our reality and guiding our actions. Ephesians 3:20 says God is able to do exceedingly abundantly above all we ask or think, according to the power that works in us. So it is important to be strong as believers and guard our minds. We have to block negative images and thoughts of fear, doubt, and failure. Thoughts that don't line up with God's word get canceled! By renewing our minds with God's Word, we align our thoughts with His promises, enabling us to live a life of victory.

3. **Create with Your Words**: In other words, watch your mouth. Make a conscious effort daily to change your negative words to positive. Instead of saying, "I can't," say, "I can do all things through Christ who strengthens me." Instead of saying, "This is too hard," say, "Nothing is too hard for God." Our words matter! Our Father God has given us an example to follow. In Genesis 1, He created the entire world with His words. Verse 3 says, "Let there be light," and there was light. Verse 6, God said, "Let there be a firmament," and heaven was created. Verse 9, God said, "Let the waters under the heavens be gathered together into one place, and let the dry land appear," and Earth was created. Our tongue is a tool. Just like our Father, we have the power in our tongue to create the life we want to see. Our very salvation was obtained by the power in our tongue, as seen in Romans 10:9: "That if thou shalt confess with thy mouth the Lord Jesus, and shalt believe in thine heart that God hath raised him from the dead, thou shalt be saved." This principle teaches us to use the creative power

of our words to speak life and blessings over our circumstances.

Throughout my life, the principles of the Success Equation—reading God's Word, meditating on it, and applying it to my life—have been my guiding force. Rooted in Joshua 1:8, these principles emphasize the importance of meditating on God's Word day and night to achieve good success. As I faced each challenge, they empowered me to overcome and emerge victorious. These tools are not just theoretical; they are practical steps that lead to tangible transformation. By integrating them into my daily life, I experienced a profound shift from defeat to victory, from despair to hope.

I want to leave you with this final truth: Every believer has a right to a life of abundance and success. You can and will experience success in life by using these three power tools within the Equation for Success. Joshua 1:8 says, "This Book of the Law shall not depart from your mouth, but you shall meditate in it day and night, that you may observe to do according to all that is written in it. For then you will make your way prosperous, and then you will have good success." This promise is not just for a select few; it is for all who choose to follow God's instructions and live by His Word. By committing to these practices, you position yourself for a life marked by God's favor and blessings.

Your story is still being written. The challenges you face are chapters that will one day be part of a greater testimony. Remember, every setback is a setup for a comeback. Keep pressing forward, rooted in faith and empowered by the truth of God's Word. We have not lost, but we continue this victorious journey. There is immeasurable power within us as we align ourselves with the word of God and partner with the victorious God who fights on our behalf. We take back our peace! We take back our joy! We take back our possessions! God restores what we thought we lost. We WIN! This victory is not just a distant hope; it is a present reality. As we stand firm in our faith, declare God's promises, and walk in His truth, we will see His power manifest in every area of our lives. Remember, the battle is already won. We are more than conquerors through Him who loves us.